Microsoft Word Exercises

Exercises for Microsoft Office Word

Authored by:

Mark Gillan MBCS MCMI MIFP MILT TQFE

Microsoft Word Exercises
Learn More

Mark Gillan

Member of the British Computer Society

Further and Higher Education College Lecturer

Teacher Qualified (Further Education)

Microsoft Certified Trainer

Member of the Chartered Institute of Logistics & Transport

Member of the Institute of Freight Professionals

Professional Photographer and Artist

Accredited Microsoft Certified Application Specialist

Certified Internet Webmaster

Member: Chartered Management Institute

skoosh media

Skoosh Media Ltd

Registered in Scotland

www.SkooshMedia.com

4 Microsoft Word Exercises by Mark Gillan

A copy of this book has been made available to:
The British Library, London, England

© 2013 Skoosh Media Ltd.

Registered in Scotland SC226730 at Head Office

www.SkooshMedia.com

No part of this book may be reproduced or stored in a retrieval system, or transmitted in any form or by any means, electronic, mechanical, photocopied, scanned, recorded, in part or complete, without written permission from Skoosh Media Ltd. The author shall not be liable for any liability, loss or damage caused or alleged to be caused directly or indirectly by the content of this book and accompanying media. This book and accompanying or related media are provided on the basis the author and publisher are not providing any legal, accounting, design, business or corporate advice, services, competent business advice or services and no other professional services except for the purposes of training without professional advice or consultation. This book is provided on the understanding the author and / or publisher will not be liable for damages for any reason whatsoever arising therefrom. Computer security is paramount and individual users, readers and anyone working with a computer must take full responsibility as it is understood by receiving this book and media, the author and / or publisher will not be held liable for any liabilities whatsoever as detailed herein or related to computer use whether through this book and media or not.

Microsoft, Word, Excel, PowerPoint, Access, Internet Explorer, Windows (all versions), screenshots and any other documentation related to Microsoft software are all trademarks of Microsoft Corporation and acknowledged. Microsoft product screen shot(s) reprinted with permission from Microsoft Corporation. This book provides independent exercises related to the use of Microsoft Office Word but this book has no affiliation with Microsoft Corporation.

All rights are reserved.

Author: Mark Gillan

Publisher: Skoosh Media Ltd

ISBN: 978-0-9557770-2-8

Microsoft Word Exercises : Learn More

For Lisa and Melissa, my friends and family, and visually impaired people around the world.

Hopefully a lot of people benefit from this book.

Author: Mark Gillan

6 Microsoft Word Exercises by Mark Gillan

Contents

- Foreword
- Book system
- Computer use
- Typing tutorial
- Typing exercises
- Exercise topics at a glance
- Important Instructions
- Exercises
- Tests—skills assessment
- Closing statement
- Shortcut keys
- Hidden "spike"
- Time savers
- List of additional tutorial notes
- Full list of exercises, topics and page numbers
- Notes
- Video media
- Answer files on media
- Additional Tutorials on media
- Additional Information

Foreword

According to my experience and office knowledge, Microsoft Word, on average is used less than 30 percent of its capabilities and will provide so much more to you after working your way through this book.

Prepare for exercises: Book System

Copy the following folders from the media provided onto the hard disk drive, external drive or any destination permitting the use of folders. Ensure folder and sub-folders are not "Read Only" after copying. (to copy—see next page)

Copy the following folders from the media:

Answers   **Complete**   **Learn**

Explanation for the folder use:

Answers folder contains all the answer files after the author has recorded video tutorials. The answer files can be used for training or comparison purposes.
Complete folder will be used for the saving of files whilst working through the book. Exercises will advise.
Learn folder contains files required for the exercises. Various types of files are provided for use with exercises.

8 Microsoft Word Exercises by Mark Gillan

Computer use

Hints, tips and short notes for computer use.

Computer / My Computer

(located usually as an icon on the desktop after booting up—Windows desktop). Double clicking on the Computer icon or accessing in any other way, provides the user with a list of drives (data areas) available. Double clicking any of the drives, including media drives such as USB flash drives or DVD/BD drives or any other drives will show folders, subfolders and files available.

Clicking on a folder will select the folder. Double clicking accesses the folder and usually the back button will mean a return to the folder shell itself. Clicking a folder, holding the shift key down and clicking another folder will select both folders and everything in between. Clicking a folder, holding the Ctrl key down whilst clicking another folder will select the clicked folders only and none in between. Right hand clicking on a selection will provide a shortcut menu with commands, including copy. Navigating using the back button and double clicking folders / drives will normally grant access … right click > Paste … delivers the copies of the selected items. So, select, copy, navigate, paste!

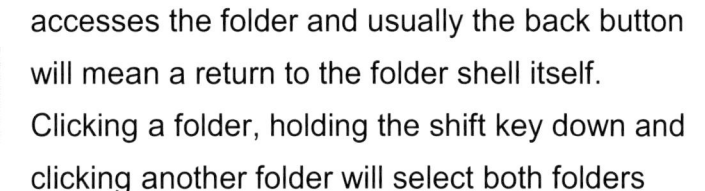

Typing

This section of the book will discuss typing to aid speed through plenty of practice. Return to this part of the book and typing exercises to build speed, ability and confidence with the keyboard.

Many people tend to use two fingers ... imagine how much time could be saved if everyone could type that bit quicker.

The Microsoft Word exercises in this book are not dependent upon speed but practice will encourage speed.

Let us have a look at the fingers on each hand. Look at the letters to which each finger is responsible and find the home keys with your index fingers on the F and J.

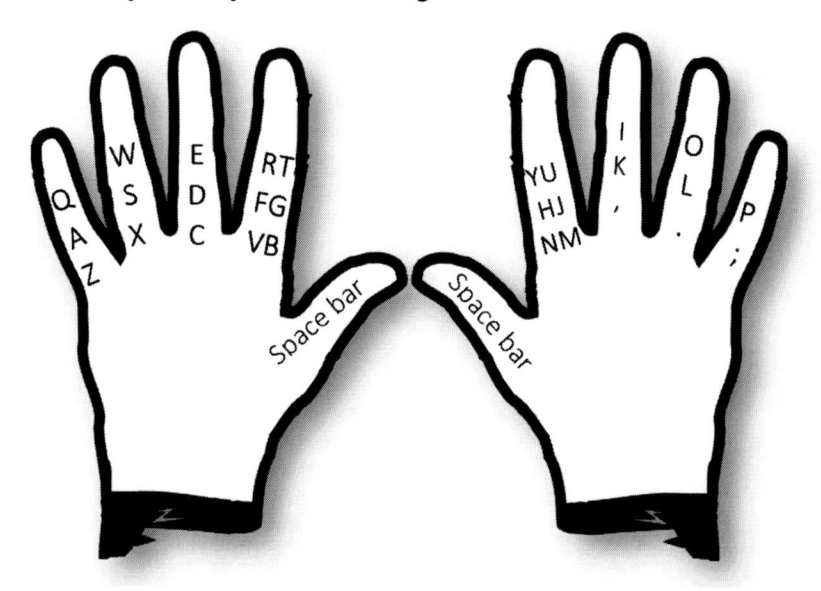

Typing Exercise A

1. Create a blank new document within Microsoft Word

2. Do not worry about mistakes or typing errors. Use the typing exercises for practice on a regular basis. Just type away into blank documents and exit when finished a session

3. Hit the space bar using your right thumb (20 reps)

4. Type the following (20 reps):
   asdfg hjkl; asdfg hjkl; asdfg hjkl; asdfg hjkl;

5. Type the following (20 reps):
   trewq yuiop asdfg hjkl; qwert yuiop asdfg hjkl;

6. Type the following (15 reps):
   zxasd zxasdfg mn.,;lkjh mn zxcvb zxcvb pq pq ty ty

7. Type the following (15 reps):
   a; sl dk fj gh asd;lk asd;lk gasd h;lk qaz p;. njvf pmqz

8. Type the following (10 reps):
   a;sldkfjgh a;sldkfjgh qaz p;. werv uion bart pokey

9. Type the following (15 reps):
   pass january quirky brilliant yellow brave craze ink

Typing Exercise B

1. Create a blank new document within Microsoft Word

2. Building upon the previous typing exercise, we will now start to type more words using various finger movements, developing keyboard dexterity and confidence. Try to think about where the keys are without looking. Refer back to the previous exercise for practice and progress forward once again.

3. Type the following words (20 reps):
   trap mown provider yarn cave went brass plate its known out our joist mountain cave moreover zebra

4. Type the following words using the shift keys with your left / right pinky and employing punctuation. Concentrate upon fingers required (15 reps):
   Comma, period or full stop. Capital letter.
   Where Would We Not Need, The World Wide Web.
   Place Over The Population, Can Bring Rewards.
   Marking Joins Us, To Provide Not Ink But Hope.

5. Type the following sentences (10 reps):
   It is fun learning to touch type using the express way.
   Providing we put time and effort into working fingers.
   Moving around the keyboard adds value to speed.

Typing Exercise C

1. Create a blank new document within Microsoft Word

2. This exercise will end the repetitions and offers practice typing from a passage using various keys. Try this exercise on a regular basis, type the following

    the quick brown fox jumps over the lazy dog (30 reps)

    Football is certainly one of the most popular games in this country, with thousands of people attending special matches every weekend but also specialized games may be played in the evening. Sports collectors seek out magazines, mugs, programmes, books, photographs, general pictures and often collections will consist of whatever is of interest related to the sport. He or she will usually source seldom available articles by reading information and using their own specialist knowledge. This usually works and will benefit them until someone beats them to the race for the most valuable and sought after items including matchboxes, playing cards, gazettes. Anything associated with the game becomes valuable through time and money is received in remuneration.

Microsoft Word Exercises : Learn More 13

Exercise Topics at a glance

Editing, Saving .... Exercises 1 thru 10

Formatting .... Exercises 11 thru 14

Other file types .... Exercises 15 and 16

Proofing Tools .... Exercises 17 thru 20

Paragraphs and Formatting . Exercises 23 thru 35

Advanced Formatting .... Exercises 36 thru 44

Styles .... Exercises 47 and 48

Referencing .... Exercises 49 thru 51

Layout and Graphics .... Exercises 53 thru 72

More referencing .... Exercises 73 thru 77

Templates, wizards, forms ... Exercises 79 thru 104

Advanced Options .... Exercises 106 thru 113

Customising Word .... Exercises 114 and 115

Assessments, Tests .... Exercises 116 thru 123

Full list of exercises, topics and page numbers at the end of the book. Additional notes and tutorials on media.

Important Instructions

Folders: As previously mentioned, the three folders (Answers, Complete, Learn) need to be copied from the supplied media onto your local computer.

Saving: At the end of each exercise, save only if requested within the exercise.

Exercise End: Close all open documents. It is best to close all open documents to avoid confusion with the next exercise or any other operation.

Individual: Each exercise is individually constructed and answered. There is no dependency upon any other exercise, making it easier for the book to be used as and when required. Ideal for learning, training, schools, colleges, universities … anywhere at all.

Layout: As the author is a qualified college lecturer, teacher and trainer, this book takes into consideration equality, diversity and various needs. Again, ideal for learning, training, schools, colleges, universities and near enough everywhere.

Files: Exercises requiring files—supplied on media.

Standards: Unless otherwise advised—A4 portrait

Exercise 1

Run, Type and Exit Microsoft Word

1. Run Microsoft Office Word

2. Type the following text using the keyboard:
   I just love using this software. Until later in the book, I will not worry about red squiggly lines or green ones.

3. Exit Microsoft Word without saving

4. Run Microsoft Office Word once again

5. Type the following text using the keyboard:
   The book is helping with my keyboard skills.

6. Exit Microsoft Office Word once again

7. Run Microsoft Office Word once again

8. Type the following text using the keyboard:
   A document will be closed in a minute.

9. Close the document without saving. Do not exit Microsoft Word just yet

10. Take a second to look at the screen without any document open but ready for more action

11. Exit Microsoft Office Word to end this exercise

Exercise 2
Saving into a Documents folder

1. Run Microsoft Office Word

2. In a blank new document type the following:
   Saving a file is very important at an early stage.

3. Save the file as **2Exer** into the documents folder as a Word document. Default settings for the folder may be the documents folder

4. Close the file, without exiting Microsoft Word

5. Request a new blank file from within Microsoft Word

6. Type the following into the new blank document:
   Saving another file into the documents folder now.

7. Save the file as **2bExer** into the documents folder ensuring the file is saved correctly

8. Exit Microsoft Word

Note: Exiting after a document change will mean Word will ask the user if the file should be saved or not. Closing or exiting a file where no changes have been made will execute the command immediately

Exercise 3
Saving into a subfolder / drives

1. In a new blank document type the following:
   Files can be saved into various places.

2. Save the file as a Word Document into the folder named **Complete** folder (see important instructions chapter), naming the file: **3Exer**

3. Close the file, without exiting Microsoft Word

4. Request a new blank file from within Word

5. Type the following into the new blank document:
   Files can be saved into other drives if available

6. Plug a USB Flash Drive / removable storage media into an available port or any other available drive

7. Save the current Microsoft Word document as **3bExer** as a Word Document into a new folder to be named **external** within the available drive

8. Exit Microsoft Word prior to removing any drive

Care: Ensure drives are removed correctly to avoid loss of data. See supplied media for removable drive instructions and tutorial.

Exercise 4
New blank document and Autocorrect

1. Close any open documents, including any blank document provided

2. View the screen with no document open

3. Request a blank new document

4. Type the following (exactly as given, including the mistakes, continue typing placing spaces where appropriate), as if a 'typo' has been made:
   Micosoft has placced an autocorrect facilitty within the sofftware to assisst with commonn mistakes made by users. It includes common typing errors and some sppelling misstakes.

5. Insert a carriage return (new paragraph) and type the following, but stop the autocorrect from correcting:
   Autocorrect would change the word wronng to wrong

6. At the end of the document, type:
   I now see how autocorrect worrks. So verry good.

7. Save your file as a word document to the **Complete** folder with the file name **4Correct** (see prepare for exercises chapter / important instructions)

Exercise 5

Typing exercise and Saving a File

1. Run Microsoft Office Word

2. Type the following text into the new blank document: Microsoft Word is truly remarkable with text processing, providing me with plenty of tools for production of letters and reports. This computer application software can take care of tasks such as mail merge, automation, insertion of graphical content and so much more! It does not come as standard and a licence must be purchased separately. When purchasing a new computer, it is wise to ask "does this PC come with Microsoft Office installed or do I have to pay extra?"

3. Insert a carriage return (new paragraph) and type the following: Word processing software will help me to perform many tasks on a daily basis.

4. Save the file as a word document with the file name as **5Exer** into the **Complete** folder

5. Close all open files—as with the end of all exercises throughout this book

Exercise 6

Opening a file, inserting text and saving

1. From within Microsoft Word, located within the **Learn** folder, open the Document named: **InputName** (see important information chapter)

2. At the end of the text within the file, type your full name

3. Save the file into the **Complete** folder which should be located within in the same place as the **Learn** folder, as a Word document named **6InputName**

4. Remaining within Microsoft Office Word, open the file named **PlaceName** located within the folder named **Learn**

5. At the end of the text within the file, type the place you live, followed by:
   It is a nice place but would like to visit many places around the world. There is so much to see in and so much to do in life. I want to enjoy!

6. Save the file into the **Complete** folder, as a Word document named **6PlaceName**

7. Close all open files

Exercise 7

Editing and Deleting text

1. From within Microsoft Word, located within the **Learn** folder, open the Document named: **humanmade**

2. Type a heading for the document on the top line by itself:
   Nearly perfect but not quite

3. Delete the last sentence of the document reading:
   What more can I learn?

4. At the end of the paragraph two, delete the wording:
   and understands
   (Ensure the sentence remains with punctuation)

5. At the end of the paragraph one, change the wording "it is classified as an input thing or something like that" to now read:
   it is classified as an input device.

6. In paragraph three, change the acronym of MDU to now read: VDU (two instances)

7. Save the file into the **Complete** folder, as a Word document named **7humanmade**

Exercise 8

Opening, Typing and Saving Practice

1. From within Microsoft Word, located within the **Learn** folder, open the Document named: **keyboard**

2. Underneath the heading of "Typewriters" type the following text:

   The original typewriters appeared more like sewing machines and very few people used them away back in 1714. The reason they looked more like sewing machines is because their manufacturer also made sewing machines, the company being Remington. Inventor, Christopher Latham Sholes developed the more modern style keyboard for a typewriter back in 1866, he patented the typewriter keyboard in 1868, with Remington mass marketing the marvellous invention in 1877.

   Due to the order of the keys they kept jamming, so James Densmore re-designed the order of the keys to slow it down and reduce jamming.

3. Save the file into the **Complete** folder, as a Word document named **8keyboard**

Exercise 9

Opening, Editing and Saving Practice

1. From within Microsoft Word, located within the **Learn** folder, open the Document named: **fantastic**

2. Within the paragraph under the heading "Fantastic", change the word "thingies" to now read: things

3. Within the paragraph under the heading "Fantastic", change the word "machines" to now read: computers

4. Within the sentence under the heading "Super", change the wording to now read:
Editing information can be done, without too much trouble when you know how it is done.

5. Within the text under the heading "Original", delete the word "and" replacing it with a comma

6. Within the sentence under the heading "Storage", replace the word "insert" with the word: contain

7. Within the text under the heading "Retrieve", replace the word "certainly" with the word: possibly

8. Save the file into the **Complete** folder, as a Word document named **9fantastic**

Exercise 10
Cut, Copy and Paste

1. From within Microsoft Word, located within the **Learn** folder, open the Document named: **Inverclyde**

2. Copy the wording: The town is called

3. Paste this wording in front of every heading, namely in front of the headings of Port Glasgow, Gourock, Inverkip

4. Near to the end of the document, locate the paragraph reading "Many important people hail from Greenock…" and by using the cut command, move the paragraph to just under wording "Important People" located at the Greenock headed part of the page

5. Every instance of wording "Thank" should have the same wording placed afterwards, to enable each instance to read: Thank you, this is the end of this part.

6. Save the file as a Word document into the **Complete** folder, naming the file **10inverclyde**

Exercise 11
Font and Font Size

1. From within Microsoft Word, located within the **Learn** folder, open the Document named: **jobformat**

2. Increase the font size to 12pt

3. Change the font for the whole document to Arial

4. Change the font for the name at the end of the document, being Joseph Origami, to now be any handwriting font to enable the text to appear similar to a signature

5. Increase the font size for the name Joseph Origami to 14pt

6. Type the following directly under the name Joseph Origami:
   Officer to the Community

7. Ensure the wording "Officer to the Community" is in Arial and increase the size to 16pt

8. Save the file as a Word document into the **Complete** folder, naming the file **11jobformat**

Exercise 12
Bold, Italic and Underline

1. From within Microsoft Word, located within the **Learn** folder, open the Document named: **memberfees**

2. The wording "Notice of Membership Changes" as a heading needs to be shown bold

3. At the end of the letter, the name of the bank needs to be shown bold

4. Underline the wording "Section 9"

5. Use italics for the wording "Care must be taken with amendments to handbooks"

6. Type your name into the space provided between the "Yours faithfully" and "Bank of Bay Leaf", using italics and bold

7. Locate the words "must be" in the first part of the letter and double underline both words

8. Change the colour of the double underline to red

9. Save the file as a Word document into the **Complete** folder, naming the file **12memberfees**

Exercise 13

Editing, Typing, Formatting Exercise

1. From within Microsoft Word, located within the **Learn** folder, open the Document named: **sport**

2. Change the main heading at the top of the document being the word "Sport" to be 30 point, bold and double underlined in red

3. Apply the font of Gill Sans Ultra Bold and font size of 22 point to the heading of: Soccer

4. Within the sentence underneath the Soccer heading, change the word "wonderful" to "beautiful" applying italics and the font colour purple

5. Under the heading of "Golf", immediately after the sentence reading "… this game…" type the following: usually has 18 holes to sink a small ball using clubs, with various terrain and obstacles.

6. Type your name at the end of the document using the font Bradley Hand ITC or Brush Script MT Italic, blue, and 18 point

7. Save the file as a Word document into the **Complete** folder, naming the file **13sport**

Exercise 14
More Formatting

1. From within Microsoft Word, located within the **Learn** folder, open the Document named: **rightway**

2. Apply font Algerian or Baskerville Old Face, to the heading "Distinct Headings" and increase the font size to 22 point with bold

3. Within the text under the heading "Distinct Headings", remove bold and underline from the word "requires"

4. The wording in the next sentence, beginning "Even subtle changes…" requires the word "subtle" to have font size increased from 14pt to 15pt

5. Within the same sentence as the word "subtle", apply italics to the word "difference" as well as 15pt

6. Change the font for the second heading "Message" from Bauhaus to: Bookman Old Style

7. Within the paragraph under the heading "Message", change the font size for the word "Small" to 12pt

8. Save the file as a Word document into the **Complete** folder, naming the file **14rightway**

Exercise 15
Saving in other file formats

1. From within Microsoft Word, located within the **Learn** folder, open the Document named: **security**

2. It is important this document should be ready for reading around the world on various computer systems and software. The file should be saved into the **Complete** folder as a Plain Text file, using the name **15security** (it is acceptable to lose formatting for the text file)

3. A new organisation has requested the file for publishing on their website but only require the file to be saved as a single file web page, into the **Complete** folder, naming the file **15web**. The web page should be named Security Advice

4. Another organisation advises they have Microsoft Office 2003 and with the file saved in a manner that will avoid any converters, saving the file into the **Complete** folder, naming the file **15older**

5. Save the original file as a Word document (most recent version) into the **Complete** folder as **15security**

Exercise 16
Opening other file formats

1. From within Microsoft Word, located within the **Learn** folder, open the Word Document named: **PhotoArt**

2. At the top of the document, type the file type

3. Save the file as a Word Document to the **Complete** folder named: **16PhotoArt** and close the file

4. From within Microsoft Word, located within the **Learn** folder, open the Plain Text File named: **PhotoArt**

5. At the top of the document, type the file type

6. Save the file as a Plain Text File to the **Complete** folder named: **16PhotoArt** and close the file

7. From within Microsoft Word, located within the **Learn** folder, open the Rich Text file named: **PhotoArt**

8. At the top of the document, type the file type

9. Save the file as a Rich Text file to the **Complete** folder named: **16PhotoArt** and close the file

10. Open the folder named Learn and take note of the size of file for **PhotoArt** for each file type

Exercise 17
Spelling and Grammar

1. From within Microsoft Word, located within the **Learn** folder, open the Document named: **spellbound**

2. Use the spelling and grammar tool within Microsoft Word, completing the spelling and grammar correction where applicable

3. Do not change the name "Gillan" as it is correct as it stands at the moment and it should be added to the dictionary to avoid the same issue arising again

4. Do not change the name "Mahoond" as it is correct as it stands at the moment (no need to add to any dictionary)

5. Ensure the tool is fully complete

6. Check the document over for correctness, especially the last few paragraphs, changing the relevant word in the last paragraph manually

7. Save the file as a Word Document to the **Complete** folder naming the file: **17spelling**

Exercise 18

Word Count and Proofing Tools

1. From within Microsoft Word, located within the **Learn** folder, open the Document named: **Celticlands**

2. Run a compatibility test to check for issues arising if the document is saved in an earlier version, such as Word 2007

3. In the space provided within the "Please note" section, type the first three words from the list of issues arising from the compatibility test check dialog box into the relevant place within the document

4. At the end of the sentence for the first numbered point at the top of page one, type the number of words contained within the document, ensuring the number excludes end notes and text boxes

5. At the end of each sentence within the numbered points found at the top of page one, type the response to the counts in numbers

6. Save the file into the **Complete** folder as a Word document named: **18Celticlands**

Exercise 19
Thesaurus and Research

1. From within Microsoft Word, located within the **Learn** folder, open the Document named: **mpm**

2. Using the Thesaurus, investigate the word "discussions" within the first line of the letter body

3. Change the word "discussions" to another relevant word

4. Also using the Thesaurus, copy another word for the word "change" within the third paragraph of the main body of the letter and paste the word into brackets after the word "change"

5. Research the country "South Africa" and insert an interesting fact into the relevant space provided within the document

6. Research the country "Papua New Guinea" and insert the number of Kilometres into the space provided toward the end of the letter

7. Save the file into the **Complete** folder as a Word document named: **19mpm**

Exercise 20
Translation and Language

1. From within Microsoft Word, located within the **Learn** folder, open the Document named: **language**

2. Each of the headings, beginning with "Language around the world" requires translating into Spanish. Just after the hyphen for each heading, place the Spanish equivalent of the heading

3. On page two of the document, the French language has been inserted as "le monde est petit". Using the translation tool, insert the English equivalent in the space provided

4. The very last line of the document on page two contains some Danish. Replace the wording "intet ændres" with the English equivalent

5. Save the file as a Word document into the **Complete** folder, naming the file: **20language**

** NOTE: If any user has problems with Microsoft Equation during the next exercise (21), try installation of Cambria Math font or try installation download the compatibility pack from Microsoft. Unfortunately a small Microsoft Word problem can exist for some users. Hope this helps!

Exercise 21

Inserting Symbols and Equations

1. From within Microsoft Word, located within the **Learn** folder, open the Document named: **mathematics**

2. In the title of the document, stating "Cost of paper 1.25", place the Euro symbol before the value.
   The Euro symbol is shown like this: €

3. Immediately after the heading "Joking" place a smiley face from the symbols insertion tool

4. Immediately after the heading "Division", place the mathematical symbol for division
   Example of symbol: ÷

5. In the space provided, within the Pythagoras headed paragraph, place the formula for Pythagorean Theorem using the appropriate tool

6. Within the last sentence of the document, place the copyright symbol and text similar to this:
   © Mark Gillan

7. Save the file as a Word document into the **Complete** folder, naming the file: **21mathematics**

Exercise 22
Summary Challenge SC1

1. From within Microsoft Word, located within the **Learn** folder, open the Document named: **summary1**

2. Locate the wording "Copyright is with the holder" and enter the copyright symbol © at the end of the sentence

3. The first line reading "Standard Material" needs to be made bold and font size increased to 20 point

4. The line reading "Courses rewarding students" needs the word "rewarding" to be shown in italics

5. Locate the word "Target" that is large in size and reduce the text to 14 point and remove the bold but make the word double purple underlined

6. Correct the spelling of the word "vectore" to now read the correct "vector" using a quick spelling tool

7. Launching the spelling and grammar tool, correct everything within the document

8. Save the file as a Word document into the **Complete** folder, naming the file: **22summary1**

Exercise 23

Strikethrough, subscript and superscript

1. From within Microsoft Word, located within the **Learn** folder, open the Document named: **sale**

2. Locate the word "second" and change it to read (ensuring formatting correct for such wording): 2nd

3. After the word "Sale" place an asterisk using superscript as shown here: *

4. Ensuring the correct formatting is used (as shown), replace the word "half" with the fraction: $^1/_2$

5. To show a reduction in the number of items available, score through the number 100 and type the following number immediately after: 92

6. After the name Patel at the end of the document, using subscript, type: Jnr

7. Save the file as a Word document into the **Complete** folder, naming the file: **23sale**

Exercise 24

Change case and other effects

1. From within Microsoft Word, located within the **Learn** folder, open the Document named: **clubentry**

2. Apply small caps formatting to the wording "Club Rules"

3. Apply all capital letter formatting to the wording "Major Notice"

4. Use the emboss formatting to emphasize the wording "Major Notice"

5. The club have every notice signed by an official but prefer to keep this text hidden. At the end of the document after "The Management" text, there is some text declaring who signed the document. Change the document to show the text.

6. Now type "no secrets here" next to the text "Major Notice" at the top of the document. Hide the text.

7. Save the file as a Word document into the **Complete** folder, naming the file: **24clubentry**

Exercise 25

Highlighting text and Font colour

1. From within Microsoft Word, located within the **Learn** folder, open the Document named: **photolaw**

2. Make the font colour red for the sub heading text: "Photographers and the Law"

3. Make the font colour green for the sub heading text of: "Questioning the legal impact"

4. Highlight in yellow, the text "not to capture images"

5. Within the last line of the document, highlight in red, the word "security" and the last word of the document being "freedom"

6. Change the font colour of the first line text from the current blue to gold, accent 4, lighter 40%

7. Remove highlighting from the pink highlighted word "recent" ensuring no highlighting upon this word remains

8. Save the file as a Word document into the **Complete** folder, naming the file: **25photolaw**

Exercise 26
Paragraph alignment

1. From within Microsoft Word, located within the **Learn** folder, open the Document named: **allstaff**

2. The text "Notice 1391 - all staff" needs to be right aligned

3. The paragraph commencing "It is essential …" needs to look more pleasing to the commercial eye by having the paragraph justified across the margins, including up to the text "… money saving vouchers."

4. Select only the example menu text (including all text within the menu being in red). Centre / center align the red text only, leaving the latter paragraphs of the document

5. Right align the name at the bottom of the document, namely "Sara Patel"

6. At the bottom of the document, left align the text "Document 1391" without disturbing any other text

7. Save the file as a Word document into the **Complete** folder, naming the file: **26allstaff**

Exercise 27
Paragraph spacing

1. From within Microsoft Word, located within the **Learn** folder, open the Document named: **spacing**

2. Provide 22 point spacing after the first line of text to separate it from the next paragraph. The first line of text is in bold and reads "Title: Using Computers"

3. It is difficult to see where each paragraph of the document begins. Identify each paragraph by its beginning text declaring paragraph number. Provide 16 point spacing after each paragraph (do not alter the paragraph spacing for the title of the document)

4. Edit the spacing for the second paragraph to provide for 18 point spacing before and 18 point spacing after

5. Insert the following text at the end of the document as a new paragraph:
Last note: Always read prior to publishing

6. Provide 22 point spacing before the new paragraph

7. Save the file as a Word document into the **Complete** folder, naming the file: **27spacing**

Exercise 28
Drop Cap

1. From within Microsoft Word, located within the **Learn** folder, open the Document named: **light**

2. To provide some artistic decoration to the first paragraph, drop cap the first letter for the word "Light" (not into margin)

3. For the second paragraph beginning with the word "In", use drop cap across 5 lines

4. For the third, apply drop cap for the first letter, using a different font of your choice, dropping across 4 lines, with a distance from text of 0.4 cm (or equivalent)

5. The fourth and final paragraph, use drop cap into the margin

6. Change the font for the drop cap in the first paragraph to be different from all other text, one of your choice

7. Save the file as a Word document into the **Complete** folder, naming the file: **28light**

Exercise 29
Line spacing

1. From within Microsoft Word, located within the **Learn** folder, open the Document named: **sunshine**

2. The address in bold within the letter is occupying too much space and line spacing should be reduced to only 1.0 lines

3. Within the body of the letter, paragraph one requires an easier read, increase to double line spacing across the whole of this one paragraph

4. The fourth paragraph requires line spacing to be exactly 20 point in size

5. Remove the space between the second paragraph and the sentence reading: "Food should be hot." (Ensure this sentence remains underneath the second paragraph)

6. Provide line spacing between "Yours faithfully" and the name "Mrs Lottie Winner" for at least 44 point

7. Save the file as a Word document into the **Complete** folder, naming the file: **29sunshine**

Exercise 30
Indentation

1. From within Microsoft Word, located within the **Learn** folder, open the Document named: **editing**

2. Apply approximately 3 cm (1.2 in) left indentation to the first word "Editing" using the ruler guide

3. To provide emphasis to the purple text paragraphs on page one, provide left indentation of 2.54cm (1in) and right indentation of 1.25cm (about $^1/_2$ inch)

4. On page two, locate the text in purple headed "Proofreading vs. Editing". Apply first line hanging indentation of 2.54cm (1in) to the paragraphs

5. The purple text on page four requires the hanging indentation to be changed to first line for 1.25cm (about $^1/_2$ inch)

6. At the end of document, on a line by itself, with left indentation of 5cm (about 2 inches), type: Wikipedia Commons

7. Save the file as a Word document into the **Complete** folder, naming the file: **30editing**

Exercise 31
Tabs

1. From within Microsoft Word, located within the **Learn** folder, open the Document named: **movies**

2. Remove spaces and hyphens between data (including headers) between the lines in the "This Issue" section and separate using left tabs at: 0.1cm (0.39in), 7.2cm (2.83in), 11.1cm (4.37in)

3. The "Information" section requires spaces and hyphens removed. List the data (including headers) using two left tabs at 1.5cm (0.59in), and at 9.9cm (3.9in) using a dotted leader

4. The countries section on page two, adjust tabs: change the second tab to be 6.2cm (2.44in), remove the bar tab, change the last tab to be 11.3cm (4.45in)

5. Funds data on page three: remove spaces, hyphens and clear tabs. Now insert: left tab at 2.22cm (0.87in) and a decimal tab for the amounts at 8.8cm (3.47in) with a dotted line leader

6. Save the file as a Word document into the **Complete** folder, naming the file: **31movies**

Exercise 32

Clear formatting and Format editing

1. From within Microsoft Word, located within the **Learn** folder, open the Document named: **initiative**

2. Clear all formatting from the first two text paragraphs

3. Edit the formatting of the address to be Times New Roman, 12 point and bold

4. Remove the bold and italics from the word "faithfully" at the end of the letter

5. Change the font for the word "Signature" at the end of the letter to now be using any handwriting font with the size of 18 point and italics

6. Change the double underline for the text "must be a priority" to now be single underline in red

7. Increase the font size to 14 point for the text "15 countries" and change the font colour to red

8. Clear formatting for the text "Increase Needed"

9. Save the file as a Word document into the **Complete** folder, naming the file: **32initiative**

Exercise 33

Text spacing and Kerning

1. From within Microsoft Word, located within the **Learn** folder, open the Document named: **yoga**

2. Apply kerning for fonts 14 points and above, for all paragraphs (the whole document)

3. For the first paragraph, apply spacing of condensed by 0.9 point and the position needs to be raised by 3 point

4. Scale the last paragraph of the document on page four to be 70% and lowered by 2 point

5. Use proportional number spacing for the numbers "123" located immediately after the title of "Yoga" at the top of the document

6. The red text "Thin Inner Happiness" needs to be scaled to 50% and condensed spacing of 1.2pt

7. In the second paragraph, locate the word "conflict" and reduce the scale from 200% to 150%

8. Save the file as a Word document into the **Complete** folder, naming the file: **33yoga**

Exercise 34

Format Painter

1. From within Microsoft Word, located within the **Learn** folder, open the Document named: **photoage**

2. Apply the same formatting used for the heading "Photo Art" to the heading "Software" (using the format painter tool)

3. Now apply the same formatting to the heading "Enjoyment" located on the last page, using the format painter tool

4. Apply the same formatting used by the sub-heading of "Pioneers" to every sub-heading in the document currently in blue and right aligned

5. Locate the sub-heading "Rights" at end of the document. Use format painter to apply the same formatting to all sub-headings currently in red

6. In the last paragraph, apply the same formatting as used by the word "batteries" to "memory card"

7. Save the file as a Word document into the **Complete** folder, naming the file: **34photoage**

Exercise 35
Summary Challenge SC2

1. From within Microsoft Word, located within the **Learn** folder, open the Document named: **sociologist**

2. Change the font for the first heading "Sociologist" to be red, uppercase, 22pt and 18 point space after

3. In the third paragraph entitled "Average", change the 's' of the wording "early 20s" to now be superscript

4. Apply 'justify' alignment with 1.2cm (0.47in) left indentation to all paragraphs (not headings) (use format painter). Do not apply to the 'skills' list

5. In the fourth paragraph headed "Majors", highlight in green the wording "through an introductory course"

6. The skills listing within the "College" paragraph: Remove punctuation and place the data into tabbed lists at 3.3cm (1.3in) and 8cm (3.1in)

7. Scale to 200% the heading "Seniors", drop cap for the word following, across 2 lines, 0.5 cm from text

8. Save the file as a Word document into the **Complete** folder, naming the file: **35sociologist**

Exercise 36

Bullet points and Numbering

1. From within Microsoft Word, located within the **Learn** folder, open the Document named: **aid**

2. The list of three items in red on page two needs numbering using Roman numerals uppercase

3. A new numbered list should be used for numbering the red paragraphs on the third page. The third paragraph in red must be number three in the list

4. The questions in bold under the heading "Consent" need a left aligned bullet point for each item, using a question mark as the bullet point symbol

5. Level 3 should now be used as the list level for the two items under heading "Implied consent"

6. The bullet list under heading "Judgment of consent" needs to be numbered as a new numbered list

7. The red and blue list items on the first page need to be a multi level bullet list, using any symbols

8. Save the file as a Word document into the **Complete** folder, naming the file: **36aid**

Exercise 37
Sorting

1. From within Microsoft Word, located within the **Learn** folder, open the Document named: **haggis**

2. The four items listed under "Alphabetical Agenda" need to be sorted into alphabetical ascending order

3. Sort the car park list into numbered descending order

4. Under the heading "Please bring", sort the list into ascending order using the header row. Sort by "Item" then by "Variant"

5. The list of races under the heading "Alterations" needs sorting using the header row into ascending order of date then descending order for number

6. On the last page of the document, the list in purple located under the heading "Associations" needs to be sorted into ascending order of number, with the current format retained

7. Save the file as a Word document into the **Complete** folder, naming the file: **37haggis**

Exercise 38
Borders and Shading

1. From within Microsoft Word, located within the **Learn** folder, open the Document named: **holiday**

2. At the top of the page, place a quick outside border around the address

3. Around the bulleted items list, place a 3D border, red, 3pt with double lines. Ensure the spacing of the border is 3pt from the text for top and bottom, 5pt from the text for left and right

4. Place a red dotted border, above and below (not any border for left and right) the text "Food should be hot."

5. Upon the "Confirmatory Form", place shading using Gold, Accent 4, Lighter 40% with Pattern style of 15% and with the RGB model apply Red 167, Green 205, Blue 141

6. Apply a standard light green shading to the last paragraph of the letter located on page two, reading "Thank you for the vacation last year …"

7. Save the file as a Word document into the **Complete** folder, naming the file: **38holiday**

Exercise 39
Inserting and Moving a Text Box

1. From within Microsoft Word, located within the **Learn** folder, open the Document named: **textbox**

2. Locate the text box at the top of the page. Change the text orientation to now be horizontal

3. Move the text box at the top of the page to have its left hand line resting at the left hand page margin

4. Insert a text box directly underneath the bold wording "Office Software" entering the following text: Microsoft Office Professional

5. Size the new text box to be sufficient to hold the text without distortion and able to read, applying a standard yellow shape fill

6. Insert a sidebar to the right, using sidebar title of: Microsoft Office Applications

7. List the following text into the content of the sidebar: Word, Excel, PowerPoint, Access, Outlook

8. Save the file as a Word document into the **Complete** folder, naming the file: **39textbox**

Exercise 40
Find and Replace

1. From within Microsoft Word, located within the **Learn** folder, open the Document named: **acaict**

2. Replace all instances of "ICTs" with the wording: Information Communication Technology (ICT)

3. Find all instances of the word "opportunities" and place emphasis upon each instance using bold

4. Change the third, sixth and thirteenth instance of the whole word "education" to now read "learning"

5. Replace all instances of the year 2012 with the current year

6. Find all instances of the word "interactive" using single underline formatting only and change the formatting to bold with italics (all other instances of the word not using underline to remain unaltered)

7. Any word ending with "ized" needs changing to now end with "ised" using Find and Replace

8. Save the file as a Word document into the **Complete** folder, naming the file: **40acaict**

Exercise 41

Paste Special

1. From within Microsoft Word, located within the **Learn** folder, open the Document named: **yogatoday**

2. The sentence: "Yoga is a path of health …" needs to be copied and pasted to the end of the document just after the word "Remember", pasting using text only without the original formatting

3. The subtitle reading "The Path to Inner Happiness" needs copying and pasting as a hyperlink after the word "Links" located at the end of the document (ensure the copied text has a working hyperlink to the original text sub title)

4. As per number 3 above. The subtitle reading "Karma Yoga" needs copying and pasting as a hyperlink within the Links section at the end of the document

5. Copy the title of the document "Yoga Today" and paste as an object using an icon at the end of the document after the wording: Dedicated to

6. Save the file as a Word document into the **Complete** folder, naming the file: **41yogatoday**

Exercise 42

Inserting a Cover Page and Page Break

1. From within Microsoft Word, located within the **Learn** folder, open the Document named: **washburn**

2. Delete the current cover page using the an efficient means for doing so

3. Just after the first paragraph of the document, read the instructions and remove the unwanted page breaks as directed within the document

4. Scroll down to the heading "Annoying" and place this at the top of a page by itself using the appropriate tool (do not use blank carriage returns / paragraphs)

5. Insert a new cover page using one of the last two available built-in cover pages

6. Insert a page break before the heading: Symptomatic

7. Scroll down and place a page break before the heading: Phenomena

8. Save the file as a Word document into the **Complete** folder, naming the file: **42washburn**

Exercise 43

Margins, Paper Size and Orientation

1. From within Microsoft Word, located within the **Learn** folder, open the Document named: **brain**

2. Change orientation to landscape for all pages

3. Change page size (paper size) to have a custom size of:
   Width: 25.4 cm (10 in), Height: 30.48 cm (12 in)

4. Change the margins to custom sized as follows:
   Left: 3.81 cm (1.5 in), Top: 3.048 cm (1.2 in)
   Right: 2.54 cm (1 in), Bottom: 5.08 cm (2 in)

5. For the last page of the document only. Change the orientation to portrait and all margins to 2.54cm (1 in) except for the left hand margin of 4.572 (1.8 in)

6. Save the file as a Word document into the **Complete** folder, naming the file: **43brain**

Exercise 44
Hyphenation

1. From within Microsoft Word, located within the **Learn** folder, open the Document named: **travel**

2. Remove automatic hyphenation from the whole document

3. Use manual hyphenation for the first paragraph within the document headed "Feet".
   The following words should be hyphenated as designated herein:

The word to be hyphenated:	As this:
habitat	hab-itat
possibly	pos-sibly
tiredness	tired-ness

4. Save the file as a Word document into the **Complete** folder, naming the file: **44travel**

Exercise 45

Summary Challenge—SC3

1. From within Microsoft Word, located within the **Learn** folder, open the Document named: **fairtrade**

2. Delete the current front cover sheet

3. Locate the list under the heading of "The main minimum criteria of FLO" and change the numbered list to a bullet list using the (character code 197) symbol: ⊕

4. At the start of the document, to the paragraph beginning "In the following chapter you will …" apply shading using the RGB model with settings of: Red 252, Green 250, Blue 184

5. Insert a cover page, using the first "built in" option (use appropriate wording of your choice to complete)

6. Replace the third instance of the word "production" appearing in bold, with the word: manufacture

7. Change the margins to "moderate" settings

8. Save the file as a Word document into the **Complete** folder, naming the file: **45fairtrade**

Exercise 46
Hyperlinks

1. From within Microsoft Word, located within the **Learn** folder, open the Document named: **resume**

2. Within the "Objectives" part of the resume document, after the word "website", insert the full address of the relevant website: http://www.europarl.europa.eu

3. Within the "Experience" part of the document, next to the Scottish Parliament entry, using the word "website" as already typed, insert a hyperlink to: http://www.scottish.parliament.uk

4. Edit the hyperlink to www.gov.ie to link to the same web address, showing the word "website" instead of the address, with a screen tip stating:
Click to see the Irish Government website

5. Within the first part of the resume, place a hyperlink for the email address and the web address as shown

6. Delete the hyperlink upon the word "material" at the end of the document, leaving the word itself

7. Save the file as a Word document into the **Complete** folder, naming the file: **46resume**

Exercise 47

Styles and Changing Styles

1. From within Microsoft Word, located within the **Learn** folder, open the Document named: **mindstyles**

2. The first line requires a title style to be applied

3. The text "H2: Science" and "H3: Method" contain formatting to which the styles Headings 2 and 3 respectively require updating to match the formatting already used upon the text (Heading 1—unchanged)

4. Apply Heading 2 and 3 styles to every relevant H2 and H3 sub-heading throughout the document

5. The paragraph commencing "The schools of Herbart…" requires the bold and italic to be removed. With the whole of the paragraph to now possess formatting of style: Quote

6. The text between the red lines needs to use a style for a paragraph list

7. Change Heading 1 to now be green and not red

8. Save the file as a Word document into the **Complete** folder, naming the file: **47mindstyles**

Exercise 48

Creating New Styles and Editing Styles

1. From within Microsoft Word, located within the **Learn** folder, open the Document named: **mind**

2. The title at the top of the document requires an increase to spacing. Edit the style being used to provide for 42 pt spacing after the paragraph

3. Edit Heading 1 style to "Keep with next"

4. Locate the text list between the red lines. This text requires a new style to be created and used based on normal style, naming the style: bullywee

5. Edit the new style as follows:
   To use bullet points symbol: √
   An increased left indentation of: 1.27cm (0.5 in)

6. A style is no longer required or used within this document. Delete the style named: OnlyBold

7. Edit the "Normal" style for the document to now use an increased font size of 12pt with 1.5 line spacing

8. Save the file as a Word document into the **Complete** folder, naming the file: **48mind**

Exercise 49
Table of Contents

1. From within Microsoft Word, located within the **Learn** folder, open the Document named: **mindtoc**

2. Check the document to ensure Headings and Sub-headings have been used throughout. Apply the relevant styles for any item remaining as "Normal" style instead of a designated heading or sub-heading

3. On the first page of the document immediately under the wording "This document contains", insert a table of contents using any of the relevant automatic tables

4. Locate the ribbon arrow containing the text "Spiritual" and "Mind". Once the outer perimeters of the graphical object is selected, delete the object

5. Locate the heading 2 wording "Soul" by using the hyperlink automatically contained within the table of contents. Select the text "Soul" and delete

6. Update the table of contents to take into consideration the recent changes to the document

7. Save the file as a Word document into the **Complete** folder, naming the file: **49mindtoc**

Exercise 50
Indexing

1. From within Microsoft Word, located within the **Learn** folder, open the Document named: **phenomena**

2. Mark all instances for indexing the following words:
   feelings (first instance within the first paragraph)
   natural (also within the first paragraph)
   mechanical (first instance in "Strive" paragraph)
   memory (first paragraph and various thereafter)
   psychology (first paragraph and various thereafter)

3. Mark one instance upon the last line of the last paragraph for the word: consciousness

4. Under the heading "Index" at the end of the document, insert an index using the following options:
   - apply one column and not two
   - right align page numbers with a dotted line leader

5. Delete the duplicated paragraph on page three headed: Experience

6. Update the index table to review page numbers

7. Save the file as a Word document into the **Complete** folder, naming the file: **50phenomena**

Exercise 51
Multi Level Lists

1. From within Microsoft Word, located within the **Learn** folder, open the Document named: **equipment**

2. Using the current list located within the document, without changing the order of the list. Allocate levels as follows using multi level bullet points:

   Highest Level: Soccer
   Next Level down: Senior and Youth
   Lowest Level: All other items in the list

3. Create the following multi level numbered list after the sentence "We need to ensure other sports…"

   ```
   1. Australian Sports
      1.1. Aussie Rules Football
      1.2. Soccer
      1.3. Cricket
   2. Irish Sports
      2.1. Hurling
      2.2. Gaelic Football
   3. Scottish Sports
      3.1. Curling
      3.2. Football (Soccer)
           3.2.1. Senior
           3.2.2. Junior
           3.2.3. Amateur
           3.2.4. Schools
      3.3. Shinty
      3.4. Golf
           3.4.1. Pro
           3.4.2. Amateur
           3.4.3. Open
   ```

4. Save the file as a Word document into the **Complete** folder, naming the file: **51equipment**

Exercise 52

Summary Challenge—SC4

1. From within Microsoft Word, located within the **Learn** folder, open the Document named: **essays**

2. Locate the word on a line by itself "Deciding" with the marking (H1) and apply style: Heading 1

3. Apply the style Heading 2, to the following words located on lines by themselves marked (H2): Sections, Timetable, Example, Ensure

4. Change all instances of style Heading 1 to now be bold, 22 point font size and font colour red

5. Change all instances of style Heading 2 to now be bold, 18 point font size and font colour dark red

6. Locate the word "Link" on a line by itself and directly after, insert a hyperlink upon new text reading "Learning", with a screen tip stating "Click this link for the learning website", whereby the hyperlink is to the website: http://www.DistanceLearning2.com

7. Upon the first page of the document, directly under the text "Essay document", place an automatic table of contents. …this exercise continued on next page...

Exercise 52—continued

Summary Challenge—SC4

8. Locate the heading "Essays (Title)" and change the style being used to a brand new style using Arial or Times New Roman font, 32 size font, bold, purple underlined and name the new style: EssayTitle

9. Apply multi level numbering to the headings throughout the document. For example:

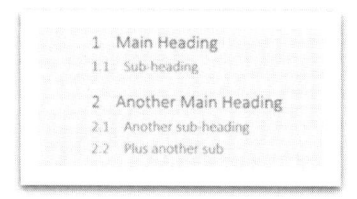

    ```
    1   Main Heading
    1.1 Sub-heading
    2   Another Main Heading
    2.1 Another sub-heading
    2.2 Plus another sub
    ```

10. Update the table of contents at the start of the document, ensuring the whole table is updated and not just page numbers

11. Mark all instances of the following words for indexing: exam … located first few words of first paragraph important … at the start of "Deciding" paragraph

12. Insert an index under the heading "Index" upon the last page of the document

13. Save the file as a Word document into the **Complete** folder, naming the file: **52essays**

Exercise 53
Columns

1. From within Microsoft Word, located within the **Learn** folder, open the Document named: **etherwind**

2. Commencing with the paragraph after the wording "Let us digest" down to and including the wording "instrument systems", apply two columns

3. Commencing with the paragraph after the wording "The idea for discussion" through to the last word of the document, apply two columns, not of equal width, left hand column being 5.08cm (2 in) and the right hand column being 8.89 cm (3.5 in), with a line between

4. Edit the document for the last two paragraphs, beginning with the text "The notion that the speed…" so that the last two paragraphs are returned to being within one column only

5. Save the file as a Word document into the **Complete** folder, naming the file: **53etherwind**

Exercise 54

Tables—converting to table, design, layout, formatting

1. From within Microsoft Word, located within the **Learn** folder, open the Document named: **colib**

2. Convert the tabular data (consisting of History, Biology, Chemistry listings) into a three column four row table

3. Within the design of the table, ensure a header row is applied. Ensure there is no difference for the first column as to any other column, leaving any row banding as it is and apply any table style of choice

4. Apply horizontal / vertical centre alignment to all cells

5. Insert a new column to the left of the "History" column

6. Apply a width of 2.54cm (1 in) to the new column

7. Merge all the cells within the new column only

8. Using at least font size of 18pt, vertical text direction (with the word commencing at the bottom of the cell), type the word "Categories"

9. Save the file as a Word document into the **Complete** folder, naming the file: **54colib**

Exercise 55
Tables—new table, formulae, formatting

1. From within Microsoft Word, located within the **Learn** folder, open the Document named: **wagesmemo**

2. Underneath the text within the memo, insert a basic unformatted three column table with 7 rows

3. Adjust the width of each cell to be 3.81 cm (1.5 in) and input the following data:

Employee:	Hours:	Salary:
J King	37.5	54,507
B Goody	42	77,412
Y Alaska	37.5	52,119
A Mann	35	32,500
M Hay	29	35,121
C Over	39	44,898

4. Insert an additional row at the bottom of the table to be designated as the total row (input: Total/Average)

5. Insert a formula to calculate the total hours for the department and insert a formula for average salary

6. Format the table using any style with total row

7. Save the file as a Word document into the **Complete** folder, naming the file: **55wagesmemo**

Exercise 56

Editing Tables, Layout, Alt text, Splitting Cells

1. From within Microsoft Word, located within the **Learn** folder, open the Document named: **tallest**

2. Delete the bottom row of the first table

3. Centre align the content of the two height columns

4. Change the table style to any other of your choice

5. Within the second table in the document, apply red shading to the "floors" column

6. Continuing to edit the second table in the document, apply cell margin across the table of:
Top: 0.25 cm (0.1 in), Bottom: 0.25 cm (0.1 in)

7. Apply Alt text to both tables as follows-
Title: Tallest Building Table
Description: Details of each tallest building

8. Delete the wording "Really Tall" and split the cell into five cells within the second table on the document, entering numbers 1-5 in each centre aligned cell

9. Save the file as a Word document into the **Complete** folder, naming the file: **56tallest**

Exercise 57
Inserting Pictures and ClipArt

1. From within Microsoft Word, located within the **Learn** folder, open the Document named: **greenock**

2. Within the space under the bold writing of "The municipal buildings" Insert the picture file located within the Learn folder named: clydetower

3. Underneath the last paragraph within the document, insert the image file located within the Learn folder named: clydepull

4. Immediately after the text "Ball games of sport", insert a clipart image of a ball

5. Save the file as a Word document into the **Complete** folder, naming the file: **57greenock**

Exercise 58

Image Size, Positioning, Cropping, Effects

1. From within Microsoft Word, located within the **Learn** folder, open the Document named: **pets**

2. The first image is considered too big, quickly reduce the size of the picture to about half the current size using the sizing handles. Now, move the picture to the right of the first paragraph and have the text wrap tight

3. The second picture of a dog requires cropping directly around the puppy. With the picture currently hiding text, move the picture to the bottom right of the text and ensure the text wraps square to the text

4. The third picture, of a rabbit, requires sizing to - Height: 5.08 cm (2 in) and Width: 7.62 cm (3 in)

5. Rotate the rabbit picture 20 degrees

6. Using the same rabbit picture, apply a 6 pt purple border around the picture, with outer shadow of your choice

7. Save the file as a Word document into the **Complete** folder, naming the file: **58pets**

Exercise 59

Shapes, grouping and order

1. From within Microsoft Word, located within the **Learn** folder, open the Document named: **stars**

2. Replace the arrow pointing to the word "star" with a block down arrow pointing to the word instead

3. Emphasis needs to be placed more upon the block arrow, place a 5-point star just above the arrow and make the star red

4. Draw a rectangle over the arrow and star but send the rectangle behind both of the other objects

5. Group the arrow, star and rectangle. Copy and paste the group of objects to have the same pointing at the red word "Important" further down the page

6. On page 2, delete the wording "Please read" and replace with an oval callout with the words "Must note" inside of the callout

7. Place a red frame basic shape behind the callout

8. Save the file as a Word document into the **Complete** folder, naming the file: **59stars**

Exercise 60
Smart Art

1. From within Microsoft Word, located within the **Learn** folder, open the Document named: **newco**

2. Below the wording "The new team is arranged …" insert a hierarchy organisational smart art chart similar to the following (formatting does not need to be the same, the structure should be the same):

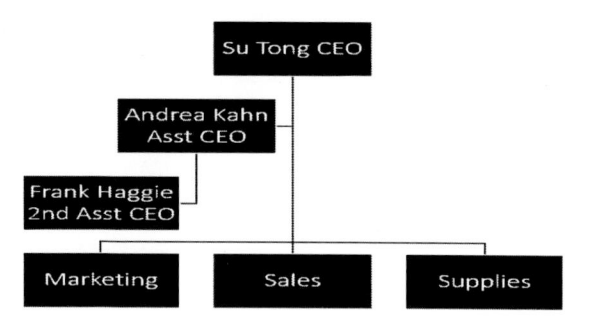

```
                    Su Tong CEO
                         |
              Andrea Kahn
              Asst CEO
              |
   Frank Haggie
   2nd Asst CEO
   |
   Marketing        Sales         Supplies
```

3. Change the layout to be:
   Name and Title Organisation Chart

4. Apply any colourful style

5. Change the shape for the top CEO position to be horizontal scroll and make it much larger than the other shapes in the chart

6. Save the file as a Word document into the **Complete** folder, naming the file: **60newco**

Exercise 61
Word Art

1. From within Microsoft Word, located within the **Learn** folder, open the Document named: **ecommerce**

2. Change the title text "Commercial Activity" into a black lettered style WordArt, applying top and bottom text wrap to the new WordArt

3. Apply a red shape outline to the WordArt, with a red glow shape effect

4. Change the heading "B2C e-commerce" into WordArt with lettered reflection, green letters and yellow outline to the letters within the WordArt

5. Change the next heading "B2G e-commerce" into WordArt with lettered shadow effect, red letters and yellow outline to the letters within the WordArt

6. Change the next heading "C2C e-commerce" into WordArt with a bevel text effect and apply a text fill WordArt text fill using RGB model with settings: Red = 231, Green = 36, Blue = 236

7. Save the file as a Word document into the **Complete** folder, naming the file: **61ecommerce**

Exercise 62
Summary Challenge—SC5

1. From within Microsoft Word, located within the **Learn** folder, open the Document named: **onsecure**

2. Place the one paragraph following the heading "Internet Services" into two columns with the left smaller than the right column

3. Immediately under the heading "Advantages" insert a three column five row chart, populating as follows:

Example Purchase	On the high street	Online purchase
Television	799	599
Hi-Fi	250	195
Delivery Cost	15	45
Total Cost		

4. Reduce the height and width of the chart, applying a table style of your choice, noting the header row, total cost row and the first column containing labels

5. Insert a formula to calculate the total costs

6. Change the main title of the document "Online Security" to now be WordArt using reflection

7. Save the file as a Word document into the **Complete** folder, naming the file: **62onsecure**

Exercise 63

Summary Challenge—SC6

1. From within Microsoft Word, located within the **Learn** folder, open the Document named: **camclub**

2. Under the heading "Member Photo" insert the picture named petnewpup located within the Learn folder

3. Flip the image horizontally and crop to discard some of the background and retaining the puppy itself. Apply top and bottom text wrap and position inline

4. Change the table to a different table style, adding a row at the bottom for totals

5. Within the new table row at the bottom, type "Totals" in the first cell of the new row and insert formulae to calculate relevant totals within the other cells

6. Locate the black square at the end of the document. This is hiding some graphical content. Send the black square to behind all other shapes

7. Group all the shapes and rotate 15 degrees

8. Save the file as a Word document into the **Complete** folder, naming the file: **63camclub**

Exercise 64

Watermarks

1. From within Microsoft Word, located within the **Learn** folder, open the Document named: **wagesecret**

2. Insert a Watermark using custom settings as follows:
   Text Watermark: Top Secret
   Font: Times New Roman or Trebuchet, Size: 44 point
   Colour: Purple, Lighter 60% or approximate
   Semi-Transparent and default Layout: Diagonal

3. Save the file as a Word document into the **Complete** folder, naming the file: **64wagesecret**

Exercise 65

Page Numbering

1. From within Microsoft Word, located within the **Learn** folder, open the Document named: **fairtrade**

2. Insert Roman Numeral page numbers at the bottom right of each page (except the cover page), with the word Page and number

3. Save the file as a Word document into the **Complete** folder, naming the file: **65fairtrade**

Exercise 66
Page Colour and Page Borders

1. From within Microsoft Word, located within the **Learn** folder, open the Document named: **electricity**

2. Apply a page colour based upon the RGB model:
   Red: 250, Green: 250, Blue: 154

3. Apply a page border with the following settings:
   Green, 3D, double line, 3pt width
   Ensure the page border is applied to the whole document.
   Also apply the following placement measurements from the edge of the paper:
   Top: 28pt, Bottom: 28pt, Left: 25pt, Right: 25pt

4. Save the file as a Word document into the **Complete** folder, naming the file: **66electricity**

Exercise 67

Themes and Effects

1. From within Microsoft Word, located within the **Learn** folder, open the Document named: **psychology**

2. Apply the theme named "Slice" or "Foundry"

3. Change the colour for the theme to green

4. Change the font for the theme to Arial

5. Apply effects named "Banded Edge" or "Opulent"

6. Save the current theme to the Complete folder, naming the theme: 67theme

7. Save the file as a Word document into the **Complete** folder, naming the file: **67psychology**

Exercise 68
Inserting Charts

1. From within Microsoft Word, located within the **Learn** folder, open the Document named: **ecogro**

2. Directly underneath the wording "Here it is..." insert a chart of type 3D clustered column chart

3. Populate the chart with the following data:

	Trees	Shrubs	Plants
Quarter 1	550	245	790
Quarter 2	324	410	823
Quarter 3	701	578	439
Quarter 4	595	292	722

4. Apply chart style 4 to the newly created chart and insert a chart title of: Orders for this year

5. Directly underneath the wording "It remains positive..." insert a 3D pie chart

6. Populate with the following data for Orders:
Trees: 1470 Shrubs: 2950 Plants: 1130

7. Apply chart style 3 to the newly created chart and insert a chart title of: Projected annual orders

8. Save the file as a Word document into the **Complete** folder, naming the file: **68ecogro**

Exercise 69

Editing a Chart

1. From within Microsoft Word, located within the **Learn** folder, open the Document named: **spend**

2. Change the top "Main Spend Channel" chart to now be a 3D pie chart, changing the chart title to now read Main Spend Zone

3. Apply a chart style to the pie chart to show percentages and separate the largest segment from the rest of the pie, changing its individual colour to red with black 6pt outline

4. Ensure the legend is shown and increase the font size to 12pt

5. Change the chart type for the bottom chart to now be a column chart, editing the title to read: Seasonal

6. Select the data and switch row / column for the seasonal column chart

7. Change the colour scheme for the seasonal chart

8. Save the file as a Word document into the **Complete** folder, naming the file: **69spend**

Exercise 70

Sizing, copying and pasting a chart

1. From within Microsoft Word, located within the **Learn** folder, open the Document named: **zoostats**

2. Copy the chart object only and paste into a brand new blank document

3. Increase the size of the chart to now have Height: 10.16 cm (4 in), Width: 15.24 cm (6 in)

4. Change the colours used within the chart to something different

5. Edit the title of the chart to now read: Zoo Lizards

6. Save the new file as a Word document into the **Complete** folder, naming the file: **70zoo**

7. Close the original Word document named **zoostats** without saving

Exercise 71
Header and Footer

1. From within Microsoft Word, located within the **Learn** folder, open the Document named: **science**

2. Delete the current footer within the document

3. Insert any header incorporating the document title, being "The Science of the Mind"

4. Insert a footer showing the page number of the amount of pages within the document

5. Aligned away from the page number, insert your own name into the footer of the document, keeping the page numbers

6. Increase the size of the font for the header

7. Save the file as a Word document into the **Complete** folder, naming the file: **71science**

Exercise 72
Header and Footer Options

1. From within Microsoft Word, located within the **Learn** folder, open the Document named: **drafting**

2. Insert any header that uses page numbers. Ensure odd pages use a different page number alignment to even page numbers. Do not have any header upon the cover page

3. Insert a footer on every even page with the text "Learning to write" with a footer on every odd page with the text "Making a draft"

4. Place an appropriate clipart image into even page footer

5. Adjust the position for the header to measure from the top of the page 2.54 cm (1 in)

6. Adjust the position for the footer to measure from the bottom of the page 3.81 cm (1.5 in)

7. Close the header and footer ribbon

8. Save the file as a Word document into the **Complete** folder, naming the file: **72drafting**

Microsoft Word Exercises : Learn More 87

Exercise 73
Bookmarking

1. From within Microsoft Word, located within the **Learn** folder, open the Document named: **guitar**

2. Bookmark the following words:

Word(s)	Location	Page Number
electric	1st line – Arch Top Guitars paragraph	4
amplified	6th line – Resonator Guitars paragraph	5
workhorse of rock	1st line – Electric Guitars paragraph	2
range	2nd line – Bass Guitars paragraph	6

3. Delete the bookmark named: Marshall

4. Insert hyperlinks upon the following, linking to the required bookmark as listed:

Place hyperlink upon word(s):	Location to place hyperlink:	Link to bookmark:
range	Page 1 – 3rd line – Acoustic Guitars	range
amplified	Page 2 – second last line of Electric Acoustic Guitars paragraph	amplified
The electric guitar	Page 2 – first line under the heading Electric Guitar	electric

5. At the end of the document, place a hyperlink upon "The Workhorse?" to link to the relevant bookmark

6. Save the file as a Word document into the **Complete** folder, naming the file: **73guitar**

Exercise 74

Footnotes and Endnotes

1. From within Microsoft Word, located within the **Learn** folder, open the Document named: **celts**

2. Locate the word "globe" located at the end of the Ireland—People paragraph on the first page. Insert a footnote explaining the following:
   Globe meaning planet earth, similar to the world

3. Edit the footnote associated with Scotland—Landscape paragraph on page two, to now read "All respect …" instead of "Some respect …"

4. Locate the initials "EU" within the Ireland—Economy paragraph on page two and insert an endnote with the following wording:
   EU – European Union, also referred to as the Eurozone for countries using the Euro currency

5. The word "Alba" within the Scotland –Landscape paragraph on page two requires an endnote with the following wording:
   Alba is Scots Gaelic for the country Scotland

6. Save the file as a Word document into the **Complete** folder, naming the file: **74celts**

Exercise 75

Bibliography and Citations

1. From within Microsoft Word, located within the **Learn** folder, open the Document named: **facilitate**

2. At each listed place within the document (marked in purple), insert the relevant citation, using the style of Harvard …

   Citation1

   Author: Petty, G., **Book**: Teaching Today, **Year**: 2001
   Publisher: Nelson Thornes Ltd **Place**: UK **Pages**: 126 - 131

   Citation2

   Author: Rogers, Alan. **Book**: Teaching Adults (Third Edition) **Year**: 2002
   Publisher: Open University Press. **Place**: Buckingham, UK **Other**: Third Edition

   Citation3

   Website: Adobe Systems, USA and globally. White Paper **published online**.
   Written by: Ellen Wagner. **Web Page**: Education – Promise of eLearning.
   Web address:
   http://www.adobe.com/uk/education/pdf/elearning/Promise_of_eLearning_wp_final.pdf
   Accessed on 17 Feb 2008 **Comments**: various visits to website thereafter.

3. Upon the very last page of the document, insert an automatic bibliography with an appropriate label

4. Save the file as a Word document into the **Complete** folder, naming the file: **75facilitate**

Exercise 76

Table of Figures

1. From within Microsoft Word, located within the **Learn** folder, open the Document named: **learntool**

2. Scroll down to the first diagram. Insert a caption reading "Figure 1—Using ICT strategies" below the illustration

3. Scroll down to the next, being a chart. Insert a caption reading "Figure 2—Chart showing inventory" below the illustration

4. Insert a caption for the next illustration, reading "Figure 3—Personal Activity" below the image

5. For the next, insert a caption reading "Figure 4—Interpretation" below the chart illustration

6. Continue to the last, inserting a caption reading "Figure 5—Learner and Teacher Analysis"

7. At the end of the document, insert a table of figures

8. Save the file as a Word document into the **Complete** folder, naming the file: **76learntool**

Exercise 77
Cross referencing

1. From within Microsoft Word, located within the **Learn** folder, open the Document named: **singing**

2. Within the first paragraph under the heading "Learning to sing", insert a cross reference after the emboldened text "born with ability -" to the bookmark named "perfect", select the hyperlink option and refer to the page number, including the below option

3. At the end of the same first paragraph, next to the text "More Info -" insert a cross reference to Table number 1—requirements, referring to the entire caption

4. Within the paragraph for the sub section known as "Just keep singing", upon the purple text "Also see the section -", insert a cross reference to the heading "Learning to sing", referring to the heading and ensuring the checkbox for hyperlink is de-selected. Again, use appropriate cross referencing wording

5. Save the file as a Word document into the **Complete** folder, naming the file: **77singing**

Exercise 78
Summary Challenge—SC7

1. From within Microsoft Word, located within the **Learn** folder, open the Document named: **needs**

2. Apply a custom page colour using RGB model, with settings of: Red 242, Green 242, Blue 180

3. Apply a red border to the first paragraph only, using a solid 1pt 3D line, removing the left and right lines

4. Use the wording "Draft only" as a watermark, selecting the font Arial Rounded MT Bold or Trebuchet or Calisto, with other default settings

5. Change the chart type for the "Disability Trend for past 4 years" to now be a 3D column chart

6. Insert a caption with a new label of "Visual Rep" reading "Visual Rep 1—Visual representation of disability statistics" for a table below the chart

7. Navigate to the next image / diagram. Insert a caption below, for a figure without the label within the caption reading "Professional Development illustration"

   continued on next page ...

Exercise 78

Summary Challenge—SC7—Continued

8. Change the colour fill to a green style for the Professional Development illustration

9. Place a bookmark named "training" at the start of the paragraph reading "CPD is most evident…"

10. Within the paragraph headed "Brookfield", place a cross reference upon the text CPD hyperlinking to the bookmark named "training", using page no before

11. At the end of the "Brookfield" headed paragraph, replace the text "quote from Brookfield" with a citation as follows:
    Book: Becoming a Critically Reflective Teacher
    Author: Stephen D Brookfield, Year: 2005,
    City: San Francisco, Publisher: Jossey Bass

12. Within the paragraph headed "Rogers", after the quotation, replace the text "quote from Rogers" with a citation as follows:
    Book: Teaching Adults, (Third Edition)
    Author: Alan Rogers, Year: 2002
    City: Buckingham, Country: UK,
    Publisher: Open University Press   …continued…

Exercise 78

Summary Challenge—SC7– Continued

13. Edit the source for Scottish Government citations to now be the year 2010 instead of 2008, altering the date accessed to now be: February 2013

14. Update the bibliography listing at the end of the document to take into account the edited source and the additional records of Brookfield and Rogers

15. After the bibliography, insert a table of figures

16. Insert an endnote for the heading "Bibliography" to read:
    Dates are for training purposes for the book

17. Insert page numbers, in the footer, including the word "page" along with the actual number field

18. Insert any style header with the words "Summary Challenge 7—Word Exercises", ensuring the header is 2.54cm (1 inch) from the top of the page

19. Save the file as a Word document into the **Complete** folder, naming the file: **78needs**

Exercise 79

Date and Time

1. From within Microsoft Word, located within the **Learn** folder, open the Document named: **jobapp**

2. At the top of the letter, insert the date today (current date) using English (United States) settings and ensure the date is updated automatically when the file is next opened. Use long form style of date, including the day itself

3. Within the paragraph reading "To evidence how keen…" replace the wording "date today" with today's date using English (United States) settings, using short form style of date but ensuring the date does not update automatically the next time the file is displayed

4. At the end of the paragraph, replace the word "now" with the actual time (current time) using 24 hour clock settings, ensuring the time is not automatically updated and is the same as the system clock

5. Save the file as a Word document into the **Complete** folder, naming the file: **79jobapp**

Exercise 80
Quick Parts and Fields

1. From within Microsoft Word, located within the **Learn** folder, open the Document named: **proposal**

2. The title of the document has already been saved within the properties of the file. At the top of the document, using quick parts / fields, insert the file property of title

3. Immediately following the text "Current status for this proposal stands as…" and also on the same line and immediately following the text "Text forming the proposal at this stage of…", insert quick parts / fields showing the file property of status

4. Insert the file property for manager from the fields list, immediately after the text "Manager…"

5. Save all the red text, including the new additions, to quick part / gallery for reuse in future similar files

6. On page two of the document, type how to save parts for future use in other documents using the gallery

7. Save the file as a Word document into the **Complete** folder, naming the file: **80proposal**

Exercise 81
Inserting an Object

1. From within Microsoft Word, located within the **Learn** folder, open the Document named: **notice**

2. Underneath the text "News just received...", as an object, insert the text from the plain text file located in the **Learn** folder, named: **kualalumpur**

3. Below the newly inserted text, insert another new object (chart) from a Microsoft Word document, located in the **Learn** folder, named: **product**

4. Navigate to the end of the document, insert an object being the Microsoft Excel file containing additional data related to the products, located within the **Learn** folder, named: **projection**
   Insert the file as a linked icon only. Do not insert the actual contents of the file and ensure an icon is shown

5. Save the file as a Word document into the **Complete** folder, naming the file: **81notice**

Exercise 82
Using a Microsoft Template

1. Create a new document using Microsoft template: Memo (Professional design)

2. Enter the following information into the memo in the appropriate places (replacing the label within each field throughout the memo document):

   Company Name: YourName Inc.

   To (recipient): Mo Ramp
   From: Your own name
   cc: (carbon copy): Professor Gillan
   Date: enter a date of your choice
   Re (subject): Template Use

3. The wording of the memo should read:
   It is important all learners commence training for the use of templates sooner rather than later. Time and efficiency is imperative. Enjoyment of computers will follow with improved efficiency and time saving.

4. Save the file as a Word **Document** file into the **Complete** folder, naming the file: **82memo**

Exercise 83

Saving as a customised template

1. Create a brand new blank document within Microsoft Word

2. Into the header of the document, type your name and address

3. Format the information within the header. Increase the font size used for your name to ensure it is larger and bolder than the address. Centre align everything within the header

4. Into the footer of the document, type your website domain address (if you have one), email address (if you have one), telephone number and any other address information

5. Exit from the header / footer

6. At the top of the document, place an empty carriage return. After the blank carriage return, insert the date in long form style (using your local date system) and ensure the date automatically updates

7. Save the file as a **Word Template** file into the **Complete** folder, naming the file: **83letterhead**

Exercise 84

Using a Customised Template

1. Open the **Learn** folder and create a new Word document, using the *template* file named: **communication**

2. Enter your own name into the space provided after the text "This template today is being used by…"

3. Immediately following the text "The message from the user is…" type the following:
   I am able to use templates and enjoy the benefits.

4. Type your name at the end of the document

5. Save the file as a Word *Document* file into the **Complete** folder, naming the file: **84comm**

6. Create another new Word document, using the same template file named: **communication**

7. Repeat step 2 above within the new document

8. Repeat step 3 above but using the following message instead of the previous: Yet another similar document

9. Save the file as a Word *Document* file into the **Complete** folder, naming the file: **84wonderful**

Exercise 85

Editing a Template

1. The Word template located within the **Learn** folder named: **interview** requires amending within Word

2. To enable to template to be used for various applications, the name Ahmad at the start of the document requires deletion

3. The invitation paragraph mentions "Old Town plant" instead of "New Town plant", change accordingly

4. Towards the end of the document, Donald Aqua needs replacing by Tupiwa Tatenda as supervisor

5. The template cannot be replaced with the same name, so save the file as a Word Template file into the **Complete** folder, naming the file: **85interview**

6. The Word template located within the **Learn** folder named: **start** requires amending in a similar manner

7. The name Donald Aqua needs to be replaced with Tupiwa Tatenda and "Old " replaced with "New Town"

8. Save the file as a Word Template file into the **Complete** folder, naming the file: **85start**

Exercise 86
Using a Template with Automated Fields

1. Open the **Learn** folder and create a new Word document, using the *template* file named: **payment**

2. Insert the following data into each of the respective fields:

   Payment being sent to …   enter: Jane Li
   Payment amount …   enter: 2457.32
   Enter 1st, 2nd, snail …   enter: 2nd
   Electrician or Plumber…   enter: Plumber
   Name of assistant…   enter: Chenguang Cuifen

3. Save the file as a Word document into the **Complete** folder, naming the file: **86janeli** and close the file

4. Once again, create a new Word document, using the same *template* file named: **payment**

5. At the same prompts as above, enter the following data in the relevant order and in the relevant dialog boxes:
   Lubna Amana, 3420.07, 1st, Plumber, Abdul Majid

6. Save the file as a Word document into the **Complete** folder, naming the file: **86lubna**

Exercise 87

Creating a Template with Automated Fields

1. From within Microsoft Word, located within the **Learn** folder, open the Document named: **goldtruck**

2. After the word "From: " at the top of the document, insert a field whereby the Microsoft Office user of the computer would automatically be entered, formatting the input using title case

3. Immediately after the text "The date today…" insert the date in your local format including the day, allowing for automatic update

4. Immediately after the text "Booking time…" insert the current system clock time in any format

5. After the text "…40ft trailer at…" insert a fill-in field with the following text (ensuring the style of strong continues into the field): New Town or Old Place?

6. After the text "Send confirmation to…" insert a field that duplicates the input that follows "…40ft trailer at…" using the copying of any text utilising the style of strong within the document

    this exercise is continued on the next page …

Exercise 87

Continuation of Exercise 87 from previous page

7. Immediately after the text "Authorised by Customer Services Management" insert a fill-in field asking the user to "confirm or state the authorisation is in progress" using the wording "Confirmed" as default

8. At the bottom of the document, insert a field that will automatically show the Microsoft Office user initials

9. Save the file as a Word *Template* into the **Complete** folder, naming the file: **87abooking** and close

10. Now try the template to ensure everything works. Using the newly saved Word template within the Complete folder named **87abooking**, create a new Word document and when a prompt arises for the fill-in fields enter the following:
    New Town or Old Place   enter: New Town
    Confirm or state authorisation is in progress, ensure the response is Confirmed
    (All other entries to the document should be automatically complete and correct)

11. Save the file as a Word **document** into the **Complete** folder, naming the file: **87booked**

Exercise 88
Working with Comments

1. From within Microsoft Word, located within the **Learn** folder, open the Document named: **world**

2. Insert a comment to the words "thirty years" within the first paragraph stating "It is certainly worth considering changing the wording to three decades"

3. Edit the comment related to the word "net" in the third paragraph so the abbreviation of "WWW" is changed to now read: World Wide Web

4. Within the section headed Revolution, to the wording "Arab Uprising" insert a comment reading: More commonly known as "Arab Spring"

5. Under the heading of Mobile phones, the comment upon the word "Anglia" is no longer required

6. Navigate to the very last comment as and add a further comment reading: Now done and complete

7. Save the file as a Word document into the **Complete** folder, naming the file: **88world**

Exercise 89
Labels

1. Create a document containing labels suitable for Avery 5160 with 30 labels per page, using a colour design of your choice

2. Input your own name and address into the label details, showing 30 labels of the same address information across the sheet

3. Save the file as a Word document into the **Complete** folder, naming the file: **89Avery5160**

4. Request a blank new default document within Word

5. Create a new label based upon Avery US Letter 3263 Postcards, changing the label height to 10.16 cm (4 inches) and the width to 12.7 cm (5 inches), naming the new label: 89NewLabel

6. Insert the following address for a full page of the same label using a New Document print option
   Moon Green Garage Supplies,
   180 Dart Avenue, Alpha City, 00141 Populace

7. Save the file as a Word document into the **Complete** folder, naming the file: **89labelnew**

Exercise 90

Summary Challenge—SC8

1. Edit the *Template* file as instructed. The template file located within the **Learn** folder is named: **oxoletter**

2. Insert the current date at the top of the document using the quick method, applying your local long form style, without the date being automatically updated

3. Replace the following words with the respective fields, adhering to each instruction:

   Word: **Replace with fill-in field asking:**
   oxofill1   Address to send the letter?
   oxofill2   Name of person to contact?
   oxofill3   Reference for company being contacted
   oxofill4   What is the Job Title advertised?
   oxofill5   Name of the newspaper running the ad?
   oxofill6   Company name with job vacancy?

4. Navigate to the text "My ref: …" and replace "oxoref" with a field that will automatically fill the name of the template file, fully complete with path and displayed in lowercase, followed with a space and the current date in short form without automatically updating

   ...exercise is continued on the next page...

Exercise 90

Summary Challenge—SC8—continued

5. Save the file as a **Word Template** file into the **Complete** folder, naming the file: **90applyltr** and close the template file after saving

6. Using the newly created template file located within the **Complete** folder named **90applyltr**, create a new document and complete the fields as follows:

   Fill-in field request ...followed by response to be inserted for this new document:

   Address to send the letter?

       Vijay Pinnacle Ajax, 101 New Street, Delhi

   Name of person to contact?

       Mrs Sneha Raj

   Reference for company being contacted

       SR/VPAHR/13

   What is the Job Title advertised?

       Plant Manager

   Name of the newspaper running the ad?

       Trumpet Toot

   Company name with job vacancy?

       Vijay Pinnacle Ajax (Services) Century

...this exercise is continued on next page

Exercise 90

Summary Challenge—SC8—continued

7. Above the text "Yours faithfully", as an object, insert all the text from the file located in the **Learn** folder named: **grateful**

8. Upon the text "Yours faithfully", insert a comment reading: Must remember to sign or insert a picture of scanned signature prior to posting

9. Save the file as a Word document into the **Complete** folder, naming the file: **90entered** and close the file

10. Create a new document containing return address labels with amount per page of your own choice and apply a design / colour / image to the labels

11. Insert the following name and address:
    >Indigo MacDougall
    >147 Red Drive
    >Swanston-on-Clyde
    >Evergreen

    Ensure all labels show this name and address

12. Save the file as a Word document into the **Complete** folder, naming the file: **90labels**

Exercise 91
Mail Merge Wizard

1. From within Microsoft Word, located within the **Learn** folder, open the Document named: **coast**

2. Invoke a mail merge using the mail merge wizard, following these guidelines:

   Use the current letter as the starting document and create a new data source with three new records (detailed below) to merge, saving the source data to the **Complete** folder as: **91datacoast**

   Dr Jamal Barakat
   121 Speakers Avenue, Greater City
   Scotland, G99 1LP

   Mrs Senga McPate
   45 Burgh Road, Loch City
   Scotland, L21 4ZX

   Dr Jolanda Ngige
   78 Skye Crescent, Alba City
   Scotland, A12 9CB

   …exercise continues on next page

Exercise 91

Continuation—Mail Merge Wizard Exercise 91

3. Place fields for the title, full name, address, city and country underneath the date at the top of the letter, without using ZIP code or any other field not listed herein. Insert relevant spaces and punctuation

4. Immediately after (on the same line) the word "Dear" insert the title and surname fields for a more formal letter to customers

5. At the end of the sentence reading "The parcel should have arrived on time at …" insert the field for city name for each record

6. Complete the merge to all records, generating a new file with the three new letters therein. Saving the new file to the **Complete** folder, named: **91mrgcoast** and close the file, leaving the original letter on the screen

7. Save the original letter file containing the fields as a Word document into the **Complete** folder, naming the file: **91ltrcoast**

8. Ensure both files are saved to the Complete folder

Exercise 92

Mail Merge using Data from a Table

1. From within Microsoft Word, located within the **Learn** folder, open the Document named: **thankyou**

2. Commence a letter mail merge using the mail merge wizard

3. The **thankyou** file already opened on screen should act as the current document for a letter, using the table within the Microsoft Word document located within the **Learn** folder, named: **teachers**

4. Edit the record for Sir Robert McGregor to change subject for this record from "Unknown" to now read: Economics

5. Match the data table fields. Match Postal Code to the relevant field and match department with subject, checking all other fields to be correct

6. Select all records for the mail merge except for one, do not use or generate a letter for Mr Albert Tatlocker as noted within the subject field for this record, the teacher retired last year

...this exercise continues on next page ...

Exercise 92

Continuation of exercise 92—mail merge using a table

7. Insert relevant fields for the address underneath the date at the top of the letter

8. Immediately after the word "Dear…" insert relevant fields to show title and surname for each record

9. Place the same fields to show title and surname for each field before the comma at the beginning of the following two sentences respectively, starting:
"…, without your help, encouragement, and …"
"…, sometimes in life, we do not let people …"

10. Locate the sentence starting "It has been wonderful how you have been a rock for me …" and place the subject field related to each record just before the punctuation (full stop / period) at the end of the sentence

11. Complete the merge to generate a new document containing all letters, saving the letters document to the **Complete** folder naming the file: **92mrgthanks**

12. Save the original letter file as a Word document into the **Complete** folder, naming the file: **92thankyou**
Do not save the data source file named teachers

Exercise 93
Mail Merge from other Data Sources and Filter

1. From within Microsoft Word, located within the **Learn** folder, open the Document named: **memosales**

2. Commence a mail merge for the memo using the ribbon buttons within Microsoft Word to generate a memo related to each record

3. Data is contained within Microsoft Excel Workbook file located within the **Learn** folder, named: **netservice**

4. Only include the records related to any customer with a contract for a term of 12 months (no other)

5. Throughout the memo replace the following items with the corresponding field as listed hereunder:
   - ooxx1   replace with the field: Technician
   - ooxx2   replace with the field: First and Surname
   - ooxx3   replace with the field: Username
   - ooxx4   replace with the field: Password
   - ooxx5   replace with the field: Mothers_Maiden
   - ooxx6   replace with the field: BirthYear
   - ooxx7   replace with the field: Occupation
   - ooxx8   replace with the field: Contact

   … this exercise is continued on next page

Exercise 93

Mail Merge from other Data Sources and Filter—continued

6. Check all relevant placement of fields throughout the sales confirmation memo

7. Complete the merge to a new document containing all of the sales confirmation / records and check there are 7 records having been used within the completion of the merge and all 7 appear within the document

8. At the end of the sales confirmation memo related to the customer named Wei Wan, insert a note reading: this customer has requested a delay of 2 weeks whilst they move home

9. Save the newly created merge completion file with all the relevant individual records on each page as a Microsoft Word document to the **Complete** folder, naming the file: **93mrgmemo**

10. Save the original sales memo file containing the fields as a Word document into the **Complete** folder, naming the file: **93memosales**

Exercise 94
Editing Mail Merge Documents

1. From within Microsoft Word, located within the **Learn** folder, open the Document named: **faraway**
   If you are asked to link to data, confirm by clicking "Yes". Microsoft Word should detect fields from a data file

2. Although the fields remain the same between the files, the data source file is currently located within the **Learn** folder named **nondata**, change the data source file to now be the Microsoft Word file located within the **Learn** folder named: **recdata**

3. Instead of the letter commencing with "To…" and member ID, change this line to now read "Dear " followed by the field for first name

4. Just below the date at the top of the letter, insert address block ensuring to match appropriate fields

5. Complete the mail merge to a new document for all records, saving the file as a Word document to the **Complete** folder, named: **94quart_mrg** and close
   Save the original letter file as a Word document within the **Complete** folder, named: **94faraway**

Exercise 95
Labels using Mail Merge

1. Using a new blank document, create labels within a mail merge using Microsoft $1/4$ page letter label

2. Merge with data (contained in a table) within the Rich Text Format file (rtf) located within the **Learn** folder named: **labmem**

3. Insert address blocks for all records except any duplicates and ensuring fields are matched for the address block to include first name, surname, street address, town / city, area code

4. Centre (horizontally and vertically) the address blocks across all labels

5. Preview, then complete the merge to a new document and save the new document containing the fully merged labels showing the individual addresses. Save the file as a Word document within the **Complete** folder, naming the file: **95memlabs**

6. Save the original file used for the merge (originally the blank file) containing the block address fields. Save the file as a Word document within the **Complete** folder, naming the file: **95newlab**

Exercise 96

Summary Challenge—CS9

1. From within Microsoft Word, located within the **Learn** folder, open the Document named: **subscription**

2. Commence a letters mail merge with the Microsoft Word document containing a list of table entries, located within the folder **Learn**, named: **subsdata**

3. Replace the text items with the fields indicated within the following list:
   ooxxoo1...replace with date, automatically updating
   ooxxoo2...replace with address block (matching the relevant fields, ensuring the correct layout is applied)
   ooxxoo3...replace with first name for each record
   ooxxoo4...replace with Subscription ID (sub_ID)
   ooxxoo5...replace with first name field

4. Complete the mail merge into a new document with all records except any duplicate and sorting into order of postal code, checking the new editable document

5. Save the new document as a Word document into the **Complete** folder, naming the file: **96subsmrg**

6. Save the original letter Word document into the **Complete** folder, naming the file: **96subscription**

Exercise 97
Macros

1. From within Microsoft Word, located within the **Learn** folder, open the Document named: **beamer**

2. Using the currently open Word document, create a new macro to be used across all future documents, named: **ending**

3. The new macro is required for the following:
   Select everything within the document
   Format the font to be Arial, 12pt, justify align
   At the end of the document, type: format done

4. Stop Macro. Ensure the macro has been named correctly and saved for use across all documents

5. Save the file as a Word document into the **Complete** folder, naming the file: **97macrec** and close

6. From within Microsoft Word, located within the **Learn** folder, open the Document named: **improve**

7. Run the macro named: ending

8. Save the file as a Word document into the **Complete** folder, naming the file: **97macrun**

Exercise 98
Editing a Macro

1. From within Microsoft Word, located within the **Learn** folder, open the Macro-enabled Word Document named: **event**
   Enable the content / allow macros for this file

2. Edit the description for the macro named "finishdoc" associated with the current document as it currently reads "Selects some text, changes the font…" and should now read: "Selects all the text in the document, alters the font …"

3. Edit the macro named "finishdoc" as follows:
   Replace the name "Hattie" with the letter "H"
   Change the name "Barbour" to be "Kerr"
   Change the name "Edvard" to be "Edward"

4. The macro named "finishdoc" contains the instruction to use the font name of Arial, change this to now be the font name of Times New Roman

5. No other changes are required, save the macro project and return to the document. Run the macro

6. Save the file as a Macro-enabled Word document into the **Complete** folder, naming the file: **98event**

Exercise 99
Protect a Document

1. From within Microsoft Word, located within the **Learn** folder, open the Document named: **salary**

2. Protect the file to ensure no-one is able to view the contents without the encrypted password that is required to be set as: promark

3. Save the file as a Word document into the **Complete** folder, naming the file: **99salary**

Exercise 100
Remove Protection

1. From within Microsoft Word, located within the **Learn** folder, open the Document named: **volunteers**

2. Unprotect the file to ensure no password is required to open or indeed any restrictions with the file whatsoever, noting the original password used to protect and encrypt the file is: volmark
(All lowercase and all one word)

3. Save the file unprotected file as a Word document into the **Complete** folder, naming the file: **100unguard**

Exercise 101
Restrict Editing

1. From within Microsoft Word, located within the **Learn** folder, open the Document named: **ceremony**

2. Restrict the document to editing by means of comments only. No other editing is to be permitted. Do not restrict anyone from viewing the document and permit the use of comments

3. Apply a password protection for the restricted editing of the document, using the password: mgaward

4. Ensure the password is input correctly—twice.

5. Save the file as a Word document into the **Complete** folder, naming the file: **101comments**

Exercise 102

Forms and Controls

1. From within Microsoft Word, located within the **Learn** folder, open the Document named: **regform**

2. Insert appropriate text input control fields immediately following each of the following:
First Name, Surname, Address

3. Insert appropriate picture content control field immediately following the text "Photograph" to enable anyone using the form to place an image file

4. Immediately following the text "Age Band" insert a drop-down list content field with choices of:
Infant, Child, Young Adult, 21-29, 30-55, 56-67, 68+

5. Insert a check box content control field before the word "Yes" and one before the word "No"

6. Immediately after the text "Registered by:" insert a combo content control field with two drop down fields, displaying initials HMcD for value: Helen McDermott and displaying initials VN for value: Viktor Nuguse

7. Save the file as a Word document into the **Complete** folder, naming the file: **102formset**

Exercise 103

Combine Forms and Protection

1. From within Microsoft Word, located within the **Learn** folder, open the Document named: **jetaway**

2. Insert a text content control field after both "First Name:" and "Surname:" respectively

3. Prior to each piece of text reading "1 month", "2-3 months" and "more than 3 months", insert a check box content control field before each item

4. After the wording of "Package:" insert a drop down list content control field to contain a selection for the following: Hawaii Gold Package, Australia, Special

5. Restrict editing to form filling, using password: jet

6. Save the file as a Word document into the **Complete** folder, naming the file: **103jetaform**

7. Close the file and reopen from the Complete folder

8. Enter data into the form as follows: Your own first name, surname, check for 2-3 months, Australia

9. Save the file as a Word document into the **Complete** folder, naming the file: **103jetbooking**

Exercise 104

Creating a form template file

1. Request a new blank document within Microsoft Word for authoring a new form template

2. Create a form using content fields as follows:
   Text: Company Name: Field: Text content
   Text: Charity? (Tick)   Field: Check box
   Text: Funding level   Field: Drop-down
   (Drop-down items: Low, Medium, High)

3. Protect the document to only allow editing of form fields and no other editing, using password: form

4. Save the file as a Word Template into the **Complete** folder, naming the template file: **104form**
   Close the file and exit from Microsoft Word

5. Generate a new document using the template file recently saved within this exercise task

6. Complete the form fields with the following data:
   Company Name: Skoosh Art, Click the check box as a charity, Funding Level: Medium

7. Save the file as a Word document into the **Complete** folder, naming the file: **104fillform**

Exercise 105

Summary Challenge—SC10

1. From within Microsoft Word, located within the **Learn** folder, open the Password Protected Macro-enabled Word Document named: **survey**
   The case sensitive password is: AuldCaledonia
   Enable the content / allow macros for this file

2. Edit the description information for the macro named "proxy" to now read: This macro inserts wording in the case of a person completing the form on behalf of someone else

3. Change the content of the macro named "proxy" from inserting the text "Your name is:" to now read "First Name:" and changing the wording "Your family name is:" to now read "Surname"

4. Place the cursor on the line below the heading of "Personal Details" and run the macro named: present

5. Insert a text content control field after the wording "Person present at meeting first name:" and a text content control field after the wording "The surname of the person present:"

exercise continued on next page ...

Exercise 105

Summary Challenge—SC10 continued

6. Insert a check box content control field before each of the responses for the question "How often do you shop online?"

7. Just before the word "Yes" insert a check box content control field and likewise a check box content control field in front of the word "No"

8. On the line underneath the question "If yes, where do you search for product information?" place a combo box content control with the following listed within:
    Search Engine
    On the high street
    Manufacturer website

9. Remove all password protection

10. Within the drop-down list control field at the end of the document (surveyor name), modify the list item reading "Asta Martin" to now read "Asta Hedegaard". Also, move "Percy Njallson" to the top of the list

11. Save the file as a Macro-enabled Word document into the **Complete** folder, naming the file: **105survey**

Exercise 106
Creating Screenshot Evidence

1. From within Microsoft Word, located within the **Learn** folder, open the Document named: **games**

2. Prepare to open another Word document and have both in separate windows, also preparing to add screenshots to the document named games

3. From within Microsoft Word, located within the **Learn** folder, open the Document named: **screen**

4. Into the file named screen under the sentence beginning "Tables Screenshot", insert a screenshot capturing the whole of the document page (reading layout / zoom) for the file named games

5. Within the file named screen, insert a screenshot clipping of only the address bar from your web browser showing your favourite web page. Ensure insertion of the clipped screenshot is under the sentence beginning "Best Web Screenshot"

6. Close the "games" file without saving that particular file but save the other file (screen) to the **Complete** folder, as a Word document named: **106screenshots**

Exercise 107
Print Options

1. The first file to open will be saved at the end of the exercise. The file will be used for screenshot recording of exercise tasks. From within Microsoft Word, located within the **Learn** folder, open the Document named: **evidence_print**

2. To perform the tasks—From within Microsoft Word, located within the **Learn** folder, open the Word Document named: **smallworld**

3. All the images within the file named smallworld are all positioned on odd numbered pages. Set print options for printing even numbered pages only

4. It might be required to print two pages per sheet. Set print options for this requirement

5. Capture a screenshot showing all the above required print options. Insert the screenshot into the "evidence_print" document underneath the heading "Print Options Complete" which yellow highlighted

6. Save the "evidence_print" file as a Word document into the **Complete** folder, naming the file: **107print**

Exercise 108
File Properties

1. From within Microsoft Word, located within the **Learn** folder, open the Document named: **bagpipes**

2. Within the file properties, set the following:

   Title: Bagpipe Maintenance Information

   Tags: bagpipes, maintenance, information, instrument, woodwind, hemping, reed, caring, maintain

   Comments: Document used for training only and will not be used in any other way. Copyright remains with the holder

   Categories: Musical, Bagpipes

   Subject: Maintenance of instrument

3. Save the file as a Word document into the **Complete** folder, naming the file: **108properties**

Microsoft Word Exercises : Learn More

Exercise 109
Accessibility

1. From within Microsoft Word, located within the **Learn** folder, open the Document named: **problems**

2. Use any tools available to ensure the document has as many accessibility issues corrected

3. Make a list at the end of the document of anything corrected or anything that could be corrected to assist with accessibility

4. Save the file as a Word document into the **Complete** folder, naming the file: **109ability**

Exercise 110
Changing the View

1. From within Microsoft Word, located within the **Learn** folder, open the Document named: **curling**

2. Change the view for the document to show multiple pages / read mode to help with the reading of the document

3. Save the file as a Word document into the **Complete** folder, naming the file: **110reading**

Exercise 111

Sharing and Tracking Changes

1. From within Microsoft Word, located within the **Learn** folder, open the Document named: **localnews**

2. Accept or Reject the changes as follows and leave a comment as instructed:

The change made:	Accept / Reject:
Age "22" to "23"	Accept the change to "23"
enquisitive friend	Reject any associated changes
"The students …"	Reject any associated changes
New Page Break	Accept the page break
CCTV	Reject any possible change
Joseph	Accept the change from "Joe"
New Page Break	Accept the page break
giggling	Reject any associated changes

3. End the process for tracking changes

4. Delete all remaining comments in the document

5. Check the document

6. Save the file as a Word document into the **Complete** folder, naming the file: **111tracking**

Exercise 112

Recovering Unsaved Files

1. Create a blank new document in Microsoft Word and type the following text:
   Recover this file if possible and if the version of Microsoft Word permits. Word 2010 and 2013 onwards allow for a temporary file to be recovered from versions but older versions of Word might require a note of the temporary file folder for Word and each file to be searched.

2. Take a note on a piece of paper as to the date and precise system time as of now

3. Exit Microsoft Word without saving

4. Oops! We needed that file!
   Run Microsoft Word once again

5. Recover the unsaved file

6. Check to ensure it is the correct file

7. Save the file as a Word document into the **Complete** folder, naming the file: **112recovered**

Exercise 113
Compare Documents

1. Open two files to compare:
   From within Microsoft Word, located within the **Learn** folder, open the Document named: **whistle**
   Also from the same location, open the Document named: **whistleirish**

2. From within the "whistleirish" file, compare the two documents, "whistle" being the original, marking all changes within a New Document with the notation: changed by Mark for exercise

3. Show all markup within the new document

4. Save the new file as a Word document into the **Complete** folder, naming the file: **113result**

Exercise 114

Customising Microsoft Word Environment

1. From within Microsoft Word, located within the **Learn** folder, open the Document named: **custom**
   (Screenshot by use of keyboard "Print Screen" button or any other means of capturing screen)
   * Insert screenshots into the relevant section within the "custom" document for each of the following tasks marked "Screenshot"

2. Screenshot: Create a new toolbar / ribbon named: special

3. Screenshot: Place the following command buttons onto the newly created toolbar / ribbon within a new group named: handy
   - Save As
   - Spelling & Grammar
   - Compare
   - Insert Table

4. Change the name of the View tab / menu to now read: SeeIt (Reset all after the exercise)

5. Save the file as a Word document into the **Complete** folder, naming the file: **114custenviro**

Exercise 115

Combining Macros with Buttons

1. From within Microsoft Word, located within the **Learn** folder, open the Document named: **button**

2. Record a macro to sign off from a document (usually a letter). The macro should:
    - Navigate to the end of the document
    - Type: Yours faithfully
    - Underneath, type your name using a handwriting font of choice
    - Underneath the handwriting font showing your name, return to the default font and type your full name

3. Insert a screenshot into the relevant space within the "button" document showing the macro code

4. Create a new button for your new macro. Placing the button either on the Quick Access toolbar or upon the standard toolbar. Assign the newly created macro to a smiley face button or a button designed by yourself

5. Insert screenshot showing the button for the macro

6. Save the file as a Word document into the **Complete** folder, naming the file: **115macbutton**

Exercise 116

Multiple Choice Questions Test—MCQ1

1. From within Microsoft Word, located within the **Learn** folder, open the Document named: **mcqone**

2. Type your full name at the top of the document

3. Type the letter of the most appropriate answer to each question after the wording "The answer is:" for each of the 10 questions

4. Save the file as a Word document into the **Complete** folder, naming the file: **116mcqfinish**

Exercise 117

Multiple Choice Questions Test—MCQ2

1. From within Microsoft Word, located within the **Learn** folder, open the Document named: **mcqtwo**

2. Type your full name at the top of the document

3. Type the letter of the most appropriate answer to each question after the wording "The answer is:" for each of the 10 questions

4. Save the file as a Word document into the **Complete** folder, naming the file: **117mcqfinish**

Exercise 118

Helpful: Creating your own Letterhead

1. Create a new blank document within Microsoft Word

2. Select the option for different first page header and footer to the rest of the document

3. Within the header, type your name using any font of choice and increase the font size

4. Remaining within the header, type your full postal address on one or two lines, using a complementary font. Ensure the font size for the address is much smaller than that used for your name

5. Navigate to the footer and in the same size font as the address had been typed in the header. On one or two lines type your telephone number, website address, email address, social networking details

6. Close the Header and Footer.
   Insert a page break and navigate to the header of the next page (changing the header but not the footer for the next page—you will edit the header and footer for any continuation pages used by the letterhead template)

    ...exercise continued on next page...

Exercise 118
Helpful: Creating your own Letterhead—Continued

7. Within the next page header, type your full name only and using a slightly smaller font than the first page header. In the same size font as the document itself (possibly the default), type the word "continuation"

8. Ensure the footer on the second page remains the same as the first page (you require your electronic contact details to appear on every page). Close the header and footer

9. Delete the page break that had earlier been inserted

11. Save the file as a Word template into the **Complete** folder, naming the file: **118Letterhead**

12. Try out the template, typing "This is my letterhead, it can be used to generate other templates based upon this one as well as documents for any purpose where a letterhead is required", inserting a page break and typing on the second page "This is the continuation sheet within my letterhead. Notice the different header and footer."

13. Save the file as a Word document into the **Complete** folder, naming the file: **118UsedLtrhead**

Exercise 119

Helpful: Creating your own form

1. From within Microsoft Word, located within the **Learn** folder, open the Document named: **jjletterhead**

2. Change the information within the header and footer to your own details

3. To allow for content within the document to be a nice distance from the header, set the top margin to now be: 4.3 cm (about 1.7 in)

4. Insert the date as an automatically updating field at the top of the document

5. Underneath the date, insert a fill-in field with a prompt reading "Name and address to send letter"

6. Underneath the fill-in field for name and address, type the word "Dear" followed by a space. On the same line immediately after the space insert a fill-in field with a prompt reading "First name or title and surname"

7. Allowing for appropriate spacing after the greeting line, type the text and insert the relevant fields:

… exercise continues on the next page...

Exercise 119

Helpful: Creating your own form—continued

7. ...continuation of number 7, type the following:

    Your invoice has been received and I have today instructed my bank to pay the amount of *[insert field for payment amount with prompt reading: enter the amount being paid]* to which I have incorporated local taxes and is in full settlement of outstanding amounts.

    Kindly confirm by *[insert another fill-in field for the recording of the communication method with a prompt reading "Type the communication method" along with a default response to prompt of "Email to my personal address"]* stating the balance of outstanding as being NIL.

    Yours faithfully
    Your Name and Your Usual Sign Off

8. Save the file as a Word **Template** into the **Complete** folder, naming the file: **119payform**

9. Try out the document fields using imaginative data, saving the completed letter into the **Complete** folder, naming the Word document file: **119xpaid**

Exercise 120

Skills Assessment 1—SA1

1. From within Microsoft Word, located within the **Learn** folder, open the Document named: **river**

2. The words "The River" at the very top of the document require formatting to the style of title

3. Find any words in the document beginning with an asterisk * and delete the asterisk, applying the style of Heading 1 to each of them

4. The word "THE" at the start of the first paragraph of the document needs to have drop cap applied to the letter "T" across 4 lines

5. Insert the page number of total amount of pages, with the word page (Page x of y) into the footer and right aligned

6. Set the line spacing for all paragraphs using "Normal" style to 1.5 and provide for 4pt before and 10pt after, with the font to be Arial and font size as 12pt

7. There has been an error with a city referenced within the file. Change any reference of "Canberra" to now read "London"   ...continued on next page ...

Exercise 120

Skills Assessment 1—SA1 ... continued

8. Within the file properties, use the following keywords to enable the file to be located during any search: river, Thames, London, plague, story, drought

9. Change the top margin to be 3.05 cm (1.2 in)

10. Make the background of every page yellow using the "RGB color model" with the following settings: Red 251, Green 249, Blue 175

11. Insert a table of contents at the very beginning of the document on a page by itself

12. At the end of the document, locate the wording "Scotland Yard" and apply a hyperlink to any online website related to "New Scotland Yard"

13. Mark for index, all instances of the following words : zymotic, hot, east, plague, deadly

14. On a page by itself, at the end of the document, insert an index

15. Save the file as a Word document into the **Complete** folder, naming the file: **120sa1**

Exercise 121

Skills Assessment 2—SA2

1. From within Microsoft Word, located within the **Learn** folder, open the Document named: **magic**

2. Change the page size from A3 to A4

3. Change the page orientation to portrait

4. Increase the line spacing for all text to 1.5 lines

5. Remove hyphenation

6. Reduce the size of the "magic" clipart image to now be the following:
   5.08 cm (2 in) in height and 3.81 cm (1.5 in) in width

7. Apply a frame picture style and rotate the image slightly around anti-clockwise. Middle right align upon the page with tight text wrapping

8. Set the margins for the document as follows:
   Top 2.54 cm (1 in), Bottom 3.81 cm (1.5 in)
   Left 1.27 cm (0.5 in), Right 1.27 cm (0.5 in)

9. Place text from "Card Tricks" (page 2) into two columns, the left hand column larger than right hand

...SA2 continued on the next page...

Exercise 121

Skills Assessment 2—SA2 ...continued

10. Adjust the columns to the following:
    Column 1 should be 12.7 cm (5 in) in width, a space of 1 cm (0.4 in) between the columns and a line, Column 2 should be the balance permitted

11. Apply Heading 1 style to any text followed by (H1) markings and delete the (H1) markings themselves

12. Apply Heading 2 style to any text followed by (H2) markings and delete the (H2) markings themselves

13. Locate the word "psychological" that appears in red bold writing. Research the word for an explanation of meaning and place an endnote upon the word with a summary of the explanation found

14. Translate the word "psychological" into Italian and place a comment at the word providing the translation using the comment wording of: this word sounds so much better in Italian and the translation is…

15. Invoke the spelling and grammar, appropriate editing

16. Save the file as a Word document into the **Complete** folder, naming the file: **121sa2**

Exercise 122

Skills Assessment 3—SA3

1. From within Microsoft Word, located within the **Learn** folder, open the Macro Enabled Document (enable macro content if security requests) named: **snacks**

2. The shapes in front of the word "friend" need to have the green arrow shape brought to the front as it is not viewed correctly.

3. All the shapes require grouping and moved into the header just to the left of the text within the header. The grouped shapes will become the logo

4. Reduce the size of the logo to around half the current size and apply a shadow effect

5. Within the tab listings under the sentence reading "Ambitions are for new products", edit the tabs as follows:

    Delete the tab at 2.54cm (1 in)
    Change the tab at 8.89 cm (3.5 in) to
    now be 7.62 cm (3 in)
    Change the last tab stop to be a decimal tab

...continued on next page...

Exercise 122

Skills Assessment 3—SA3 continued

6. Remaining within the tab listing area, the word "Raisins" needs the same formatting as the word "Strawberry"

7. The "signoff" macro has the incorrect job title due to promotion and needs changing to now read: Department Chief Operator

8. Immediately underneath the text "The current situation is..." run the "table" macro to insert a table

9. Delete the third and last column in the table

10. Populate the table appropriately with the following products and production amounts:
Salt Crisps - 57012, Nuts - 71344, Dips - 110354

11. In the bottom row of the table, type "Average" into the left hand cell and insert a formula to calculate the average for the production amounts

12. Format the table using an appropriate table style and using colourful formatting

...continued on next page...

Exercise 122

Skills Assessment 3—SA3 continued

13. Insert a 3D clustered column chart to graphically represent the current production as noted within the newly formatted table

14. Change the colour for each of the columns to be Purple, Yellow, Green

15. Apply data labels to the chart columns

16. Move the legend for the chart to the top of the chart plot area increasing the font size slightly

17. Add "alt" information for the logo as: "logo for fake eatery and now accessible" using alt title: "logo"

18. Change the date and time at the top of the document to only show the date in your local format with automatic updating

19. Run the "signoff" macro

20. Spellcheck the document, changing any spelling errors such as "promissed" should be "promised"

21. Save the file as a Macro Enabled Word document into the **Complete** folder, naming the file: **122sa3**

Exercise 123

Try it out

1. Create a calendar. Save the file as a Word document into the **Complete** folder, named: **123task1**

2. Create a letterhead. Save the file as a Word Template into the **Complete** folder, named: **123task2**

3. Create a new menu / tab with a selection of buttons and take a screenshot, pasting the screenshot into a new blank document. Save the file as a Word document into the **Complete** folder, named: **123task3**

4. Create a simple document consisting of a list of your groceries / household shopping to print and take with you. Save the file as a Word document into the **Complete** folder, named: **123task4**

5. Design a web page using Microsoft Word. The coding could be cleaned up by a professional web designer but you can still have fun! Save the file as a Web page into the **Complete** folder, named: **123task5**

6. Make a to-do list with check boxes and confirm jobs as and when done. Save the file as a Word document into the **Complete** folder, named: **123task6**

I hope you have enjoyed using this book and working your way through the exercises. The learning process is much easier "doing" rather than spending all your time being told how to do something.

The learning process within this book is extended to the video tutorials, additional notes and looking through the answer files.

I know the book is being used for training purposes but also for assessing candidates, training needs analysis and other personal, business, corporate, training, educational (schools, colleges and universities). Hopefully you will tell your friends, family and everyone else to buy a copy!

Quite often I hear how my hard work has helped others, whether through donations to worthy causes or from my book readers. We all like to hear how we have made an impact in the world and I am no different to everyone else in this respect. To know I am making a difference makes it all worth the great deal of effort.

The next few pages within this book contain a list of topics and their respective page number. I have also included some helpful hints and tips...as much as possible for you.

All the very best for the future and bye for now, *Mark*

Useful Shortcut keys

Here is a wee list of useful shortcut keys for Microsoft Word, with some pointers and helpful tips for you.

Shortcut keys:	Purpose / Description:
Ctrl + n	New blank document
Ctrl + o	Open a document command
Ctrl + s	Save a document
F12	Save a document as (Save As)
End	Move cursor to the end of a line
Home	Move cursor to the start of a line
Ctrl + End	Move cursor to the document end
Ctrl + z	Undo the last action
Ctrl + c	Copy selected text / object
Ctrl + v	Paste the copied text / object
Ctrl + Enter	Insert a page break
F1	Help facility
Alt + F4	Exit Microsoft Word

A hidden Spike

The hidden "Spike" tool in Microsoft Word is similar to a virtual spike sitting on your desk, whereby snippets of information can be moved and spiked. When you are ready, all of the snippets can be moved into the one place, creating a new document containing all the pieces from various other documents or from various areas of the one document. A very handy hidden tool to know all about.

To use the "spike" tool:

Select some text.
Press **Ctrl + F3** keys on your keyboard.

The text has now been moved onto the "spike" and now…

Select other text. Press the same keys as previous.

Continue until ready to empty the "spike" to the one place.

To move everything from the "spike" into a document, press **Ctrl + shift + F3** buttons.

Note: The above process moves text (not copy) and the latter part of the process empties the "spike" but it is possible to keep the "spike" with its contents by typing the word spike into a Word document and then hitting enter (as per the bubble instructions that should appear).

Time Savers

TIP: Typing a hyphen three times followed by a carriage return will insert a light solid line from left to right margins.

Typing three of the following symbols and hitting the carriage return button will also insert lines from the left to right margins but differing styles of lines:

Symbol:		Line created:
Hyphens	---	───────────────
Underscore	___	▬▬▬▬▬▬▬▬▬▬
Equals	===	═══════════════
Hash	###	▬▬▬▬▬▬▬▬▬▬
Asterisk	***	■ ■ ■ ■ ■ ■ ■ ■ ■ ■
Tildes	~~~	∿∿∿∿∿∿∿∿∿∿

TIP: Macros are excellent for repetitive tasks.

TIP: Quick Parts / Building Blocks are excellent for saving regularly used text or parts of documents.

TIP: Typing * then a space followed by a list item will have the asterisk automatically changed to a bullet point upon hitting the carriage return for a new paragraph (or new list item). As with any autocorrect item, backspace will tell Microsoft Word to leave the item as it was before the autocorrect kicked in.

TIP: To create dummy text to practice using a tool, type the following and hit enter: =RAND(x,y)

Replace x with the number of paragraphs, y is sentences

List of tutorial notes on media

Included on the media are some additional tutorial notes to assist with knowledge. Teachers, trainers, lecturers, professors and many others will hopefully find the tutorial notes useful for hand-outs.

Please feel free to use but do not alter anything as this would contravene copyright.

We hope the following helps you…

- Bullets and Numbering
- Columns
- Cover Sheet
- Header and Footer
- Index
- Inserting Images
- Keep with next
- Mail Merge
- Mail Merge PowerPoint presentation
- Page Break
- Paragraph Spacing
- Password Protection
- Spelling and Grammar
- Styles
- Symbols
- Table of Contents
- Tables – Auto Tables
- Tables – Quick Tables
- Editing of Tables

The additional tutorial notes are provided for recent versions of Word, although you should find them useful for future versions of Microsoft Word with media updates

Microsoft Word Exercises : Learn More

Index of Topics and Page Numbers

Exercise Topic: .... Page:

1	Run, Type and Exit Microsoft Word	15
2	Saving into a Documents folder	16
3	Saving into a subfolder / drives	17
4	New blank document and Autocorrect	18
5	Typing exercise and Saving a File	19
6	Opening a file, inserting text and saving	20
7	Editing and Deleting text	21
8	Opening, Typing and Saving Practice	22
9	Opening, Editing and Saving Practice	23
10	Cut, Copy and Paste	24
11	Font and Font Size	25
12	Bold, Italic and Underline	26
13	Editing, Typing, Formatting Exercise	27
14	More Formatting	28
15	Saving in other file formats	29
16	Opening other file formats	30
17	Spelling and Grammar	31
18	Word Count and Proofing Tools	32
19	Thesaurus and Research	33
20	Translation and Language	34
21	Inserting Symbols and Equations	35
22	Summary Challenge SC1	36
23	Strikethrough, subscript and superscript	37
24	Change case and other effects	38
25	Highlighting text and Font colour	39
26	Paragraph alignment	40
27	Paragraph spacing	41
28	Drop Cap	42
29	Line spacing	43

156 Microsoft Word Exercises by Mark Gillan

Exercise Topic: .... Page:

30	Indentation	44
31	Tabs	45
32	Clear formatting and Format editing	46
33	Text spacing and Kerning	47
34	Format Painter	48
35	Summary Challenge SC2	49
36	Bullet points and Numbering	50
37	Sorting	51
38	Borders and Shading	52
39	Inserting and Moving a Text Box	53
40	Find and Replace	54
41	Paste Special	55
42	Inserting a Cover Page and Page Break	56
43	Margins, Paper Size and Orientation	57
44	Hyphenation	58
45	Summary Challenge—SC3	59
46	Hyperlinks	60
47	Styles and Changing Styles	61
48	Creating New Styles and Editing Styles	62
49	Table of Contents	63
50	Indexing	64
51	Multi Level Lists	65
52	Summary Challenge—SC4	66
53	Columns	68
54	Tables—converting, design, formatting	69
55	Tables—new table, formulae, formatting	70
56	Editing Tables, Layout, Splitting Cells	71
57	Inserting Pictures and ClipArt	72
58	Image Size, Positioning, Cropping, Effects	73
59	Shapes, grouping and order	74
60	Smart Art	75

Microsoft Word Exercises : Learn More 157

Exercise	Topic:	Page:
61	Word Art	76
62	Summary Challenge—SC5	77
63	Summary Challenge—SC6	78
64	Watermarks	79
65	Page Numbering	79
66	Page Colour and Page Borders	80
67	Themes and Effects	81
68	Inserting Charts	82
69	Editing a Chart	83
70	Sizing, copying and pasting a chart	84
71	Header and Footer	85
72	Header and Footer Options	86
73	Bookmarking	87
74	Footnotes and Endnotes	88
75	Bibliography and Citations	89
76	Table of Figures	90
77	Cross referencing	91
78	Summary Challenge—SC7	92
79	Date and Time	95
80	Quick Parts and Fields	96
81	Inserting an Object	97
82	Using a Microsoft Template	98
83	Saving as a customised template	99
84	Using a Customised Template	100
85	Editing a Template	101
86	Using a Template with Automated Fields	102
87	Creating a Template with Automated Fields	103
88	Working with Comments	105
89	Labels	106
90	Summary Challenge—SC8	107

Microsoft Word Exercises by Mark Gillan

Exercise Topic: .... Page:

91	Mail Merge Wizard	110
92	Mail Merge using Data from a Table	112
93	Mail Merge - other Data Sources & Filter	114
94	Editing Mail Merge Documents	116
95	Labels using Mail Merge	117
96	Summary Challenge—CS9	118
97	Macros	119
98	Editing a Macro	120
99	Protect a Document	121
100	Remove Protection	121
101	Restrict Editing	122
102	Forms and Controls	123
103	Combine Forms and Protection	124
104	Creating a form template file	125
105	Summary Challenge—SC10	126
106	Creating Screenshot Evidence	128
107	Print Options	129
108	File Properties	130
109	Accessibility	131
110	Changing the View	131
111	Sharing and Tracking Changes	132
112	Recovering Unsaved Files	133
113	Compare Documents	134
114	Customising Microsoft Word Environment	135
115	Combining Macros with Buttons	136
116	Multiple Choice Questions Test—MCQ1	137
117	Multiple Choice Questions Test—MCQ2	137
118	Helpful: Creating your own Letterhead	138
119	Helpful: Creating your own form	140
120	Skills Assessment 1—SA1	142

Microsoft Word Exercises : Learn More   159

Exercise Topic: .... Page:

121	Skills Assessment 2—SA2	144
122	Skills Assessment 3—SA3	146
123	Try it out	149

Final note:

The media enclosed within the back cover of this book contain exercise files for each of the independent exercise, tutorial notes for teachers / learners, video tutorials, answer files for reference and plenty of additional material.

It is intended the media will be updated and will keep abreast of new technological advancements.

Therefore, it is recommended this book is purchased again in the future to not only furnish you with more recent versions of word processing packages but also to assist charitable organisations around the world.

The author will donate part profits to charity and will try his utmost to assist others.

If you would like to contribute in any way, please contact the author, whether you would like to gift funds, donate products / services, provide tutorials to share, assist others or indeed just to keep in touch ... the author would love to hear from you.

Appreciation:

The author, Mark Gillan, would like to say a big "Thank You" for the purchase of this book and to wish you all the very best with its use.

Useful websites:

www.SkooshMedia.com   www.ArtSale2.com

www.Photographer2.com   www.MarkGillan.com

www.CanvasPrintsSale.com   www.StopSmoking2.com

www.ExcelExercises.com   www.Hypnotism2.com

www.JockTheArtist.com   www.Ebook-Ebook.com

Remember—prior to using media:
The following folders contain:
- Learn—all the files necessary for exercises
- Complete—this folder is where to save completed files
- Answers—contains all the completed answer files
- Video—movie tutorials for every exercise
- Additional—more information, tutorials and extras

Copy the Learn and Complete folders onto your hard disk drive ready for working through the book.

skoosh media